D0849931

Give Them Stones

Mary Beckett

Give Them Stones

BTB
BEECH TREE BOOKS
WILLIAM MORROW
New York

Library of Congress Cataloging-in-Publication Data
Beckett, Mary, 1926–
Give them stones.
I. Title.
PR6052.E284G5   1987   823'.914   87-22979
ISBN 0-688-07562-2

Printed in the United States of America

First U.S. Edition

1 2 3 4 5 6 7 8 9 10

BᴛB

The word "book" is said to derive from *boka,* or beech.
The beech tree has been the patron tree of writers since ancient times and
represents the flowering of literature and knowledge.

'When they ask for bread don't give them crackers as does the Church, and don't, like the State, tell them to eat cake. Explain that man cannot live by bread alone and give them stones.'

Nathanael West, *Miss Lonelyhearts*

Give Them Stones

one

When they shot that boy in both legs up against my wall I was in the house sitting at the fire by myself. I jumped because the noise was so near and so loud, and then I ran out on to the dark street to see what was happening. Two men in balaclavas were holding his shoulders up against the wall in the lamplight and he was crying, 'Don't do it again. Don't, don't. Oh Mammy, Mammy I'm going to be good.' Another man stood over him with a gun and they delayed, keeping him there in the wet, holding him, and him crying. I shouted at them what did they think they were doing and then they shot him in the other leg and ran away.

People came out from the street behind and told me, 'Martha, ring up the ambulance. You're the only one with a phone.' My fingers took a long time to make the dial work and when I came out again they had put blankets over him and a cushion to lift his head from the wet and the dirt. Old Mrs Holmes had towels in her hand for fear of bleeding. There was very little blood. He had fainted but he groaned now and again and he was very white. 'Who is he, Martha?' somebody asked me and I shook my head because I couldn't make myself speak.

'I know his mother,' Mrs Holmes said. 'She's no good. If you sent for her now she wouldn't even be in.'

His features were thick and ugly the way some boys are when they're not children any more and haven't settled into men. The night was cold and the rain started again. The soldiers didn't come out of their billet that used to be the canning factory although they must have heard the shots. A whole crowd arrived when they heard the ambulance and watched them loading him in.

When they had all gone I brought out buckets of water and a yard brush and washed and washed at the place although indeed there was little sign that anything had happened. All the time I was brushing I was telling myself that I couldn't keep quiet about this. I had kept my head down long enough, so careful of myself, frightened of any change, never taking any risks. But I'd have no respect at all for myself if I didn't let them know what I thought. I'd tell them they were getting no more from me in their weekly collection and I'd tell them why.

In bed I wasn't so brave and I thought that maybe he had been tormenting old people, this boy, and maybe with no police in the district it was the only way to deal with trouble-makers. If they had shot him only the once I might have persuaded myself of that but I lay awake with his crying in my head. Sometimes it changed when I went half asleep, to Lizzie McAteer when I was at school, crying for her mammy while the teacher slapped her and slapped her on her thin blue curled up hands. His rough white face changed back and forward to the way she looked, all purple and blotchy, after she'd stopped screaming. And my hair had felt then too as if it were standing on end with horror.

two

At home we were reared very gently. I had heard children talking about being beaten. I had seen women pulling at their children and slapping bare legs with their hands. It never happened to us. Most of the time my father minded us because he couldn't get work. My mother and my grandmother worked in the linen mill on the front of the road. We lived in my grandmother's house. The whole row is ready to be knocked down now. A few years ago the government people painted all flowers on the gable wall and then somebody battered a hole right through them and the slates slid off year after year. So they're fit for nothing but demolition even though the priest said they should not be wrecked. 'We might be glad of them yet if there's another bout of burning,' he said. They weren't great houses; a kitchen with a black fireplace and a gas ring and a cold tap at the sink, two bedrooms upstairs, a flush toilet at the bottom of the yard, and a wee room off the kitchen where I slept with my granny.

Some people said she was a bitter old woman. I even heard my father muttering that to my mother when he didn't know I was listening and my mother stood up for her, 'Ach, Seamus, she has her good points and you have to make allowances.' That was because her husband, my grandfather, had a job red-leading in the shipyard in 1921 when the Protestants chased all the Catholics out of the Island and he went off to America on the assisted passages and never wrote and never came back. She said he was dead but she didn't know. She said he couldn't bear people thinking he was afraid. The Protestants used to jeer, she said, 'Yez all run away like rats,' they'd say and that Teague was the Irish word for rat. He was never afraid of anything in his life, she said, and nobody argued with her but we were all afraid of her tongue and I used to wonder if he had been too and was that the reason he left and never brought her out to America. Later on I heard that he drank.

When I grew too big for the cot and Mary Brigid had to move into it, I slept in my grandmother's bed until she died. If I wakened during the night I'd hear all the gurgles of her stomach and little plops of wind coming up. I hated that and kept stiff right over from her in the bed. As well too, she sighed and prayed, 'Our Lady of Sorrows, pray for us,' over and over again. One night I couldn't bear it any longer and I touched her shoulder and said, 'Granny, maybe he forgets how to write. It's hard to remember all the letters.' I was learning to write myself at the time. 'What's that, daughter?' she said and when I repeated it, feeling very timid, she said, 'You're a good wee girl. Go to sleep now,' and she tucked me up and gave me a kind of a half-hug. I was called Martha after her and she was always telling me we were the ones to get things done and it was just as well we were there because nobody else showed any signs of putting things in order.

That wasn't true, of course. My mother and father were very good. You'd never have thought my mother was tired after her day's work. She'd wash her face under the cold tap and brush the lint out of her hair and she'd spend the night sewing dresses for me and Mary Brigid and the neighbours out of remnants of cloth my granny would buy for a few pence. There wasn't a lot of cooking to be done on the gas ring – a kettle to be boiled for tea or a pot of potatoes for the dinner. Sometimes my mother would bring home sausages for us and steak for my father but then there was a row because Granny complained he shouldn't get it since he wasn't working. On Sunday mornings we'd have a fry of bacon and eggs and fried soda farls or potato farls. My mother would say to Granny, 'You'll get heartburn if you eat that potato bread,' and Granny would say back, 'And I'll get heartburn if I don't eat it.' Then afterwards she'd sip hot water with a spoonful of baking soda in it and screw up her face at the taste of it. My father lit the fire first thing every morning, winter and summer, and washed the floor as soon as they were gone to work. He didn't do the semicircle on the pavement outside the front door – Granny did that. She'd kneel down with the bucket of suds and her floor-cloth inside the door and she'd sweep her cloth round in a semicircle on the ground. It used to delight me to see how true and symmetrical it turned out each time – not just at our house but at nearly every house in the street. My father washed dishes and clothes but he wouldn't go messages, although that didn't matter once I was old enough because I was very good at doing messages. He didn't let me go to school until I was over six but he taught me at home to read and write and do sums and then I helped him to teach Mary Brigid – or that's what he said I did. He tried to teach Danny later on but Danny would never stay still long enough to learn and he had to be sent to school.

The school was a narrow blackened brick building at the end of another street of houses a bit over from ours. It had tall windows with big wire grids all over the outside of them and grey stone steps inside. There was a smell off it, a smell of toilets, a smell of wet coats, a smell of dirty children. When the school-attendance officer called at our house and said I had to go as I was turned six, my father took me by the hand and we went to see the Principal. She had black hair and orange lipstick and a wrinkled powdery face. I had heard she was cruel. My father explained to her that he had taught me so that I could go straight into first class and skip infants. She brought out a lesson book and gave me a page to read. It was about Fergus and his rabbit lost in the snow. She asked me what 'But in vain' meant and I was able to tell her but when she told me to spell 'field' I put the vowels the wrong way round and I got all red when the teacher said, 'So, fathers can't teach you everything, can they?' But she said they would try me out in first class if I was there at nine o'clock on Monday morning.

We were always up early because the mill workers had to start at eight and after they were gone my father pulled a wooden chair over in front of the fire, scraping it along the red tiles, and put our enamel basin on it. When he had poured water from the kettle into it I put my hands down spread on the bottom of the basin where it was still smooth and white with no black chips and took comfort from the warmth. He washed my face and arms and then my hands with a pink bar of soap and dried them, and then lifted me up to stand in the soapy basin while I clutched his shoulders and he rubbed up and down my legs. He started to sing, 'I have a song to sing, oh!' and then he said, 'Come on, Martha, your turn,' and I wobbled out, 'What is your song, oh?' and we both sang, ''Tis the song of a merry maid moping mum whose sight was sad and whose glance was glum,' and then we did a run of la la's all mixed up and he hugged me and lifted me into Granny's lumpy armchair to dry my feet and legs and put on clean white socks. Then he said, 'Don't tell any of the wee girls I washed you. Sure you won't.'

The teacher in first class was young and smiling, her face pink and white. Miss Farrell she was called and she had to give up teaching a few years later because of a collapsed lung. She brought me in by the hand and said, 'So you're Martha Murtagh. I've heard about you. You're the clever wee girl who learned her lessons all by herself.' I was going to tell her that my daddy had taught me but I thought maybe he wouldn't like me to tell that either so I said nothing until she admired my dress and said it was just like her milk jug at home only my blue and white stripes went up and down, hers went round the jug. I was very happy to tell her my mammy made it. 'So she's a dressmaker?' Miss Farrell asked and she lifted up the hem and examined the sewing and I said, 'No, she just makes our dresses at night.' She was good to us all and her classroom was shut off by a big wooden door from the rest of the school so we were happy enough but I used to notice her tremble when the head teacher, Miss Killeen, came into the room.

I finished the story about Fergus and his tame rabbit that wanted to be a wild rabbit but learned his lesson in the snow and was glad to get back to his cage. I was very proud of my reading. We used to pitch our voices high and think we were getting rid of our Belfast accents. 'Talking swanky' was what we called it. I read out loud to myself and one night I was doing that when my two uncles were in. They were my mother's brothers – one married, living in the next street, and the other my granny's youngest son Joe who had no job either but he was not married so he got no dole at all. He had lived in our house first but after being in England working for a while he went to live with Uncle Jimmy even though they never agreed with each other about anything. Joe was listening to the story and then he said to me, 'Give us a look at your lesson book, Martha.' I stood leaning against his knee while he read it and I wondered why he was getting so excited. When he'd finished it he said, 'Seamus, don't you see what they're filling the kids' heads with? Is it the Church or the government gets this fixed up?' and he looked at the publisher's name on the first page but he was none the wiser and my father laughed at him and handed the book over to Uncle Jimmy. Joe said, 'Don't you see what it's telling them – you're safer in your cages. Don't even try to break out or you'll be sorry. Capitalist cages and the good kind master.'

He was always talking like that. He had a bit he had found in one of my father's books. He was never done saying it.

'When they ask for bread don't give them crackers as does the Church, and don't, like the State, tell them to eat cake. Explain that man cannot live by bread alone and give them stones.'

It stuck in my head, mainly, I suppose, because I didn't know what it meant.

'Don't be annoying the child,' my father said, 'there's no call for her to be thinking the likes of that.'

'She'll never learn younger,' Joe said. 'Anyway I remember when she was born in the General Strike in January 1926 I was sent out to see could we borrow a wee bit of coal to keep the new baby warm. And everybody who could manage at all gave some even though they knew there was no coal coming in until the strike was broken and the poor divils had to go back and work for less money.'

'What are you talking about?' Uncle Jimmy interrupted him. 'They're only Englishmen. What do we care what work they have or what pay they get. They're only Englishmen.'

'They're workers,' Joe said and they were squaring up to each other as usual with their eyes standing out in a temper. 'I saw the way they're treated last year when I was over. They're no better treated than us.'

'It's their country,' Uncle Jimmy said. 'They run it whatever way they want but they have no right to keep us down. We should be in the Free State.'

'All the same,' Joe said, 'I was glad of a job in England. I had a bit of money in my pocket.'

'Why didn't you stay?' Uncle Jimmy said, all thick and cross.

'The job packed up. You know it did. There's no work there much either. I'd go back in the morning and never come back to you looking for charity if I had my fare. I'd never ask you for anything in this world. You'd never see me again.'

Then Granny told them both to stop fighting, that they were not like grown men at all, and she was fed up listening to them, and they didn't know what it was like to be tired out after a day's work. They said then they were going down to the corner and asked my father was he coming. He shook his head. He never went and stood at the corner. At nearly every street corner a group of men would stand all day because they had nothing better to do. Sometimes they played cards or shove-ha'penny, but mostly they just stood and talked. Here and there a man would have a greyhound with him on a tight leash with a big broad collar round its skinny neck and a red or grey coat on the dog even though the men themselves had no coat – just a suit and a cap and a white muffler to cover the fact that they had no clean collars for their shirts. They smoked Woodbines. When my father never joined them I thought it was because they spat and used bad language. He said it was because he was a countryman. He'd stand at a crossroads but not at a street corner.

He came from a place in Co. Armagh called College Land which I always thought was a queer name. I never was there. He had a sister, a teacher up in Dublin, far older than he was. She sent him money sometimes. Then his mother had a whole line of babies who died at birth, until my father was born when she was in her forties and she died when he was twelve. Later on he was sent up to Belfast to learn to be a barman. He lived in an attic bedroom above the pub and had to spend his days out in the yard washing bottles in cold water so he didn't like it at all and when the pub was burnt out by the Protestants in the Troubles and the publican and his family went off to Monaghan he never tried any more to be a barman. Then he was put in gaol for being in the IRA, and that's where he met Uncle Jimmy and so married my mother. But that's all I ever knew about his time in gaol because he never talked about it at all. I never heard if he was in the IRA, or if he even did anything or if it was all a mistake. He certainly never belonged to any organisation after I was born. He wasn't out of the house long enough. The only time he joined the men at the street corner was in the Troubles of 1935.

They began on the 12th of July when the Orangemen were on their way home. My father had taken Danny and Uncle Jimmy's two boys up the Cave Hill to look for bilberries. He was very keen on walks. Sometimes we'd go up a stony lane to the quarry with the spring, kneeling down on the stone at the side and lifting the water in our hands. When Uncle Jimmy's boys were there they tried pushing and shoving but my father didn't allow them to be rough with Mary Brigid or me. Then we'd walk up the heathery slope the opposite side from the caves and round the curved top of the quarry and over to the Nose. Once I was in the bottom cave, how I can't remember, but it was dirty and damp and had been used as a toilet. The Nose was really called MacArt's Fort, my father used to tell us and it was like all these forts; it was a place with a great view that could let people long, long ago see for miles if an enemy or invader was coming and be safe unless the enemy managed to climb up and if they tried they were beaten off. And not so long ago Wolfe Tone had addressed a meeting of United Irishmen up there and told them Ireland was going to be free. I didn't like the stories about tribes attacking or being besieged but I loved listening to how Ireland was going to be free. I'd look off down Belfast Lough with the ships in it and the shipyard with the gantries and over to the little hills in Co. Down and Bangor with the yachts in front of it and I'd think wouldn't it be lovely if it was really our own country that we could be proud in, instead of being kept in cramped little streets with no jobs for the men and sneered at by the people who deprived us. It was as if we were all in prison looking out at a beautiful world we'd never walk free in.

Other days we went up the Hightown Road to the labourers' cottages in the dip between Cave Hill and Squire's Hill. It was just a trudge, up, up all the way, but one of the cottages had a shop and we'd beg, 'Daddy, can we ask the man for a drink of water?' He had a bucket of water in his kitchen that he'd carried from a pump so we knew we'd have to be bought lemonade. Then my father and he would talk about the weather and the state of the country and neither of them had Belfast accents, both countrymen. Coming down the hill when the others all ran on in front, I'd take hold sometimes of my father's hand but if Mary Brigid or Danny took his other hand I'd let go. I don't know why. It used to puzzle him and he'd ask me why I did it. He'd even try to keep my hand but I couldn't stay. I had to pull away.

On the 12th of July Mary Brigid and I didn't go that time because it was a holiday from work and Mammy was at home. Granny hadn't been well and though it was a sunny day she sat in her chair by the fire with a shawl round her. When the shawl slipped down at the back she'd lift it up by stretching her arms, holding it out wide and swinging the front of it one side over the other so that the smoke billowed out of the fire. The shawl smelled of smoke and just of being worn for years. They were too heavy and black to wash, those shawls, with nothing but the sink and one tap and a little line in the yard. Some of them smelled of snuff and then they would make you choke but my granny never took snuff. My mother didn't wear a shawl ever, though it would have kept her warmer than the thin coat she wore year after year. She was a very neat woman; everything about her was neat, even the way her mouth was shut with the corners held in and up. I hated later on the way her upper lip grew wrinkles. I blamed the false teeth all the women got under the free health scheme after the war. But sure I have the same wrinkles now myself and I hate them too. She never complained, never scolded, didn't talk much at all, just let everyone else talk away. The noise she made was with the sewing machine night after night. It was a big old machine that we didn't really have room for in our kitchen so at meal-times it was pushed into Granny's bedroom where I slept. It had been given to her by an old woman who lived in our street who could no longer use it. She was an Austrian woman and had a cuckoo clock. Mary Brigid and I used to love the cuckoo clock but when Mary Brigid imitated the foreign way she spoke my mother told her to stop it at once, that her way of talking was as good as ours. Often she didn't know what we said either. The machine was on a little table that had fancy iron supports and a treadle. The top of it, the black shiny part, was decorated with gold leaves and flowers, covered when she was finished by a big wooden lid with a black iron handle. People put books and papers on top of that so every time she wanted to sew my mother had to clean it all off. She made bright flowery cotton overalls for herself and Granny. They wore dark old skirts and blouses underneath and then got into these overalls like into a sleeveless coat and folded them over the front and tied them at the back and then smoothed them down the skirt with both hands. They were always clean so they needed a lot of washing and ironing, and because the cotton was cheap they often shrank. I think of my mother at that time when I smell new cotton and remember new dresses being pulled over my head. They had no zips then, at least not in our part of Belfast, and with long-waisted dresses it was sometimes hard to pull the second arm through the armhole while fitting them on. I used to panic at times when I was stuck but my mother was patient and soothing. She smiled at Danny more sweetly than at either of us, though. I often used to think,

19

'Mammy just loves Danny.' But maybe it was because he was the youngest and full of life. She smiled at my father too, and he at her (in a way I couldn't understand until I grew up and then I envied them). She worried about Granny. She didn't smile at her so much. I thought then that if she didn't have Granny to worry about she'd have more smiles for Mary Brigid and me.

That day she tried to get her to bed but Granny just said sourly that if she lay down her heartburn would get worse, so my mother said we'd go out and buy her a few peppermints. We went to Jenny O'Neill's shop that she had in the front window of her house in the next street. A woman was coming out with a grim face and we stood back smiling at her but she just nodded. 'What's up with Lily?' my mother asked and Jenny O'Neill said, 'I hear there's shooting down in York Street.' My mother threw up her hands and said, 'My God, Seamus!' and Jenny said, 'What in heaven's name is he doing down there today?' and my mother said, 'No, no, they're up the Cave Hill.' I was amazed at my mother for not being sensible as usual and Jenny laughed at her and I laughed very loud too, but my mother was flustered and anxious and couldn't remember what she'd come for until Mary Brigid and I told her. Jenny gave us a sweet each and told us, 'Keep an eye on your mammy. She's working too hard.' She ran half of the way home, not bothering about us at all, and when she opened the door she said, 'Mammy!', a name I'd never heard her call her mother before and never heard again until Granny was dying. But Granny was asleep in the chair so we didn't waken her, just put the peppermints on her lap.

The police came and took Uncle Jimmy away that night and a few other men in the district and although they didn't come near our house my mother worried all summer. In some districts houses were burnt and people moved with a few sticks of furniture they could salvage to an airy new estate where each house had a garden, between our street and the mountains. And in every morning's paper we could see headlines about people being shot. Men were shot standing at street corners and my father took that time to go and stand with them. Every evening after our tea, instead of helping my mother round the house or reading his paper, he went down to the group at the corner where our street met the main road. On the opposite side of the road were Protestant streets – not very different from ours except there were not as many children and the doors and windows were more often shut, and better painted. It was summer and we had no school and no lessons but we weren't allowed out after the tea no matter what friends called at the door for us. Danny was always begging to go out but he was never let. My mother refused quite sharply and my father would back her up in his reasonable voice and my granny would threaten him, 'Sit down and be good or I'll give you a good scudding.' Mary Brigid and I used to laugh because she never touched any of us but Danny would glare at her. Towards the end of the summer sometimes three or four days would pass with no shootings and people would begin to let out their breath. Then it would start up again. Granny said as soon as it was peaceful and looked like being over, some policeman would take out his gun where nobody would see him and shoot off all his bullets down an empty Protestant street to provoke them again. Uncle Jimmy's wife used to come round and say nasty things about my father not being lifted by the police and when she was gone my granny would say, 'I used to like Sadie. I can't think what's got into her. Isn't Jimmy safer in there than most places? At least she knows where he is.' Joe had gone to England again and she didn't hear from him very often. When the winter came or things quietened down, Uncle Jimmy came home but his family were never so friendly with ours again, and none of us liked to see policemen in our street – big imposing men with beautiful quality uniforms and rich leather holsters for their guns and their batons.

At that time I used to read comics lent to me by Uncle Jimmy's boys: the *Hotspur* and the *Rover*. My father brought books home from Smithfield that he got for a penny or two but very few of them I could read – *Scenes From My Study Windows* and *A*

Military History of the French Revolution were two I kept for a long time without reading. In the comics there were long written stories then, not just pictures, and many of them were about the Wild West. The 'Bads' used to ride into town and terrorise the respectable citizens. They shot up the streets and wrecked saloons and the people just cowered until some hero against overpowering odds was able to get rid of them. I remember saying to my father, 'But, Daddy, hadn't they got the police in those days?' and my father laughed a bit and said he supposed not in those out of the way places. But after the riots of 1935 I thought we hadn't got the police either and two years later in the next street something happened to confirm that idea.

A boy had joined the British army as plenty did because there was no work for them at home or in England. He came home on leave and because he didn't like the army or the discipline or the early rising he didn't go back when his leave was up. The police were told to bring him in and when they were at the front door in the dark he jumped out of the back window and ran into the entry and down the next street. The police chased him and shot him dead. We heard the shots and my father rushed out to see what was going on. He was angry and white in the face when he came back. I heard him come in and I climbed over my granny in the bed and went into the kitchen but I was ordered back, only told that a boy had got himself shot. The next day people said that the police had beaten him up when they caught him and only in the end shot him. There was an enquiry later on and the policemen swore that one running with a gun in his hand had tripped on a kerbstone and shot him by accident.

I had to go over to the Falls Road to do a scholarship examination that day with five other girls. I have no recollection of the examination or the building but when we came back to our district we called into the dead boy's house to say a prayer for him. He was laid out in the wee room off the kitchen, the same as Granny and I slept in, and, in spite of all that has happened since, I can still see his face blotched yellow and green. We knelt down and I tried to concentrate on the words of the Hail Mary but my mind was shouting, 'Oh Daddy, oh Daddy,' and when I came home and he wasn't in I went out to the lavatory at the bottom of the yard and got sick.

I didn't tell them at home where I'd been and my mother said I wasn't to sit any more examinations since they made me sick but I didn't heed her and I went in for the City Scholarship, which everybody said was never given to Catholics, and Fortwilliam and a typing academy called Orange's. The school on the Falls Road gave me a scholarship but I didn't take it because I thought we had not enough money and also because school had become intolerable to me.

By that time I was in the principal teacher's class – Miss Killeen's class. And Miss Killeen was mad! I can think of no other explanation for her rages, even though my mother used to say there was a very thin line between bad temper and madness. She used to stamp the high heel of her shoe right through the floorboards and screech at the class and bang her cane on the blackboard, on the desks or on any girl who came under her notice. It was this madness in her that made poor Miss Farrell tremble when she came into her room. She was too gentle to last very long there. She left teaching altogether but I did hear that after a few years as an invalid she got married and lived happily ever after. After we left our safe haven with her we were moved out into the main school where all the rooms opened out of one another and had thin partitions in between so that no one had security. Some of the teachers were kind but unhappy and others were nearly as bad as Miss Killeen. There was an old bandy-legged teacher with rimless glasses who twitched her nose like a rabbit to keep them in place, but she shook poor wee girls when she was asking them did they do something or other and when they were terrified and said yes she said, 'And you have the cheek to admit it!' and slapped them. Another who left to get married while I was in her class was lazy. She sat at her table all day and to keep draughts away from her she stuffed rolled-up stockings in the gap under the partition. She set homework but only looked at the books of the two girls who came from the better-off corner of the parish. When girls failed to learn a lesson quickly enough or well enough to please her she lifted them up off the floor by their cheeks.

But Miss Killeen was the evil genius overall. She worked hard, to give her her due. We were hardly ever let out of her class until after four o'clock. On winter evenings we went home cold and miserable by lamplight. We sat for scholarships to all the schools she could think of to give opportunity to any who could take it. As well as that we spent a lot of time at drawing and singing. We had drawing homework night after night, and I'd cry to myself and rub out what I'd done and try again. I could never make the two sides of a jampot of flowers stand straight or get the perspective right on a pile of slanty books or boxes. We learned all about horizontal and vertical and parallel lines. In singing we learned part songs and descants and rounds and for some strange reason she was fond of hunting songs so that for months we'd be singing, 'Tally-ho, tally-ho, tally-ho!' from one part of the choir while another part would sing words about horses and hounds and foxes and jumps. Generally we had never been to the country; some of us thought that the corn was cut in the fields with scissors. And we had to plough through these songs while she bared her teeth and banged the blackboard where it was all written up in tonic sol-fa. We learned Shakespeare – *The Merchant of Venice* in fifth class and then in Miss Killeen's *As You Like It* and *Macbeth*. We were expected to prepare it at night and know what it all meant for reading-time the next day. 'What's a halberdier?' she asked the class standing in a semicircle when we came across the word one day. 'What's a halberdier? What's a halberdier? What's a halberdier?' slapping each one because none of them knew it. My hand was up and Phil McKenna's because my father had brought home a dictionary once among his books from Smithfield, and I had been able to whisper the meaning to Phil standing beside me but she wouldn't ask us till she had slapped everybody else so that half the class was crying for the rest of the time.

But the instance that horrified me beyond all the others

happened to a girl out of fifth class, not Miss Killeen's at all. There was an award then called the Carlisle and Blake Memorial Prize for the best-run school and Miss Killeen wanted to get it. To that end, we brought in furniture polish and rubbed it into the worn deal desks and Brasso for the inkwell lids so that there was always a smell of these things mixed with dirt and damp and the smoky air coming in through the tall sooty windows. She wanted to buy maps for the walls but there was no money. Catholic schools did not get as much money then as the Protestant ones and our parish was too poor to make up the difference. She showed us how she would back them with butter muslin and tack slats of wood top and bottom so that they would hang nicely on the walls. So to get the maps the teachers held raffles.

Miss Killeen was the first and she bought for it a wee brass chest of biscuits. It looked beautiful – an imitation of a pirate's treasure chest with a curved lid and hoops of thin dark wood over it. There were four little circles for it to stand on of the same dark wood as the hoops. She brought it all round the school herself and the children were delighted just to look at it, and the tickets were a penny each. Then it was put in the place of honour on a shiny half-moon table standing at the side of our class between the two doors where our room led to the others. At home-time the classes were coming through two abreast on the way out – we were still working away at the geography of the Balkan states – but there was a back-up because the only door out of the school led to steep stone steps and children naturally slowed down there. In our room the neat rows merged into a knot of people and the table was knocked and the little chest slid off the polished surface, burst open and spilled biscuits and snakes of crinkled red paper over dirty shoes and the muddy floor. There was a silence and Miss Killeen marched down with her cane in her hand. 'Who pushed that box?' she shouted and girls pointed at Lizzie who was terrified and stammering, 'Miss, I never.' Then Miss Killeen grabbed her by the wrist and jerked her hand out and slapped her and slapped her and then took the other one and did the same on it until both her blackish-blue hands were all curled up and Miss Killeen straightened them out each time with her own hand before slapping her. Lizzie was sobbing and crying, 'Mammy, Mammy,' and then started to scream and Miss Killeen pushed her over against the wall, and began to pick up the biscuits and arranged them neatly in the box. We were there standing in our seats or out on the floor gaping but we didn't do anything. My skin was all goosepimples with horror. Two or three other teachers had come in but nobody stopped Miss Killeen. Why didn't a crowd of us jump on her and pull her away? Why didn't the teachers take her by the arm? It wasn't until the biscuits were cleared up and half the girls had slipped off home that Lizzie's own teacher, white in the face, helped her to her feet, bent and shaking and still crying, and brought her to the infants' yard where there was a sink.

'Her granny'll be up tomorrow to Miss Killeen. Wait till you see. She'll pull the hair out of her.' That's what the other girls said and I was in dread of that too. I hated those scenes. But nobody came up. Nothing happened. I saw Lizzie two days later looking no different. And like the poor mean-spirited cowed people we were, we brought in our pennies and Miss Killeen bought the maps and put them up and everybody who came in admired them and she got her Carlisle and Blake Memorial Prize.

So when I was given a scholarship to the school on the Falls Road I said no I wasn't taking it, I was leaving school as soon as possible. I knew that meant two and a half more years of Miss Killeen but I didn't think a different school would make any change. Then the nuns sent for my father to try to persuade him to let me go. He told us about it when he came home. He said he was very embarrassed because the nun told him he was not to worry about money. There were past pupils that she could see about giving me their uniforms and books so that wouldn't cost anything and there were even funds that would provide my busfare across to the Falls. She said that I had written in the test a composition about going up to the labourers' cottages just before Christmas and listening to *Adeste Fideles* on the old man's wireless while my father and he talked, and looking down on Belfast with all its lights as if it was a Christmas tree, and that the English teacher had told her when she corrected it that I wasn't to 'be lost sight of'.

My father said, 'If I was earning myself I'd see to it that you took your chance and went to that school,' and my granny said, 'Well, you're not and you've never worked and there's no sign of you working and I'm not going to last for ever and you'll need Martha's pay.' I began to say he had worked every now and again but he stopped me and my mother just pushed a seam through her sewing machine and said nothing at all. So I didn't go.

Mary Brigid did though, two years later. She was always so pretty, Mary Brigid, with bright blue eyes and rosy cheeks and a lovely neat nose and mouth. Her mouth never got the lines round it the way my mother's did and mine. My mother's eyes were grey and always worried except when she made them smile. Mary Brigid wasn't like my father either, but he said she was like his mother who had died before he grew up. I didn't like him saying that. She had curly brown hair with fair bits in it when she was a wee girl, but my mother always kept it cut short. 'Why don't you let her curls grow long and golden?' I asked because I liked descriptions like that in books. 'Because her face is small and you'd never even see it if we didn't keep her hair cut,' my mother said and she was right. Mary Brigid always kept it short – all her life. Now it's silver. I was never jealous of her prettiness – I just loved looking at her.

My granny had died by that time and Mary Brigid and I slept together in her bed. Up to that she slept with my mother and Danny with my father. I can't say I mourned my granny much. She was a trouble to herself and to everybody else. But my mother was very upset and I didn't like to see that; it was so different from her usual demeanour. Every night while we were saying the family rosary she'd start to cry, control herself, and then break down again. This went on for weeks and I'd pray off and on all day, 'Don't let Mammy cry at the rosary tonight. Please help her to get through it tonight.' Apart from that Mary Brigid and I were very happy in our little room. We slept with our arms round each other and we talked long after we got into bed. When she got her scholarship she said she was going to take it, she didn't care where they got the money from with Granny's pay gone. She went round to the next street to a girl who had left that school at fourteen and bargained for her school uniform. On the Sunday war was declared Mary Brigid and I were sitting on our bed darning Granny's old black woollen stockings for her to start school the next day. The thunder was brattling and my father was saying that it didn't matter much about school because we'd likely be all killed before the end of the year. We were giggling because we were nervous and excited and my mother was making black-out curtains for half the street.

Of course we didn't get killed and Mary Brigid went to school in peace and told me every night about the quiet nuns in their long white habits and big rosary beads, and the polished floors and friendly girls.

'Outside the classroom window, Martha,' she said, 'there's a tree with a silvery stem and all delicate leaves and when I look at it I think I'm asleep and having a beautiful dream and that any minute I'll wake up and find myself back with Miss Killeen.' One night when I was dropping off to sleep I felt her crying and I sat up and shook her. 'Mary Brigid, is it all gone wrong? What's the matter? Has it turned out like Miss Killeen?' She said no that wasn't it at all but I should have been there too instead of missing it all, the lessons and the kindness and the singing in the white chapel. I told her not to be silly, that I had made up my own mind and I'd be left school the next Easter and I'd be earning money and I was just glad school was so nice for her. I thought to myself even then that I had chosen wrong but I had decided for myself. I was tempted to think that if my mother had spoken up for me I could have gone all right, or if my father was not so given to not having his way. Anyway it was over and done with and I was leaving school at fourteen like all the other children who had no money.

At this time my father had a labouring job because there was work beginning all over the city. One day Danny said all the boys were pro-German because the Germans had brought work and anyway they were going to beat England, our real enemy. My father said if we didn't like England occupying our country why should we like Germany occupying Poland? Danny looked uncomfortable and my father told him he should think things out and not just repeat what other people said. Danny would have argued but my father just read the paper and didn't answer him, didn't even seem to hear him – not a bit like himself, but I suppose he had a notion what was going to happen.

He was taken away by the police early one morning shortly after that with Uncle Jimmy and other men and interned in an old boat on Strangford Lough. My mother never complained, never missed a day at work until she had a baby four months later. It was a wee boy but it died the day after it was born.

I had started work in the mill and the woman in charge of me was kind – always telling me how great my mother was. I didn't like the noise of the machinery or the steam that filled the air to keep the linen moist. I didn't like the loud hoarse voices of some of the women or the roughness of the girls who pushed and shoved at one another because it was so hard to hear anybody talking. To begin with I told myself I'd get used to it, but after a while the thought of spending the rest of my life there made me despair. When I realised my mother was expecting a baby (she never mentioned it herself) I began planning how I'd offer to give up my job and mind it. I knew there was a woman down the street who minded babies for working women, but I persuaded myself that I'd be better although I knew nothing at all about looking after babies. When the baby died that notion had to be done away with. I'd come home after my day's work and look at myself in my father's shaving mirror over the sink and my face would be grey with bad air and tiredness and I'd look at my mother dreary and distant and I'd pray that something would happen to change my life.

I was a year working when the blitz happened on Easter Tuesday in 1941. It was a beautiful clear night with a full moon when the sirens went and we all huddled together in the kitchen. Mary Brigid and I clutched each other and said our rosary out loud to try and stop hearing the explosions and the planes and the collapse of buildings all over our end of the town. I swore I'd never complain about the mill again if we got out of this alive. Danny kept on saying he'd go out and see what was happening so my mother held on to him even though he was twelve years of age. At one stage I thought the house was wrecked when the door and front window blew in and the upstairs ceilings came down. At daylight the planes went away and we made my mother sit in Granny's chair while we brushed up the plaster and broken glass. Danny helped for a while and then he slipped out.

He came back telling us that houses were wrecked two streets away and people killed and whole blocks of houses down on the Protestant side of the road. He said he'd heard the Protestants saying that the Pope was in the first plane to show the Germans not to bomb Catholic streets. My mother got up and said we were going to the country. I thought she was gone mad because she had been so strange since the baby, and I said where could we go, where would we sleep. We'd go to two old aunts of hers near Lough Neagh, she said. I had never heard of them and when I asked questions I was told, 'Give my head peace!' We gathered up our nightclothes and walked over broken glass and gritty dust. Lorries were being loaded up with people anxious to get out – I saw Phil McKenna that I was friends with at school. She climbed into one of the lorries and I never laid eyes on her again. At the Smithfield bus station we got a bus for Aghalee just as we came to the entrance. Mary Brigid and I slept in the bus so we were able to enjoy our walk from Aghalee along little country roads with white blossoms on the hedges and across a wee rounded bridge on a canal. It was like a fairy story with the birds singing and a blue sky. Every now and then my mother would stop to get her bearings.

The aunts were sisters of my grandfather who had gone to America. Maggie and Bessie Lavery were their names because neither of them had married. They lived in a thatched cottage like the ones we used to draw for Miss Killeen in school, with a farmyard and hens picking in it and geese that ran out and attacked Danny's legs so that he kicked at them. Mary Brigid ran round behind my mother and clutched on to her and I slipped into the door and met two old women coming to see about the commotion. I thought to myself, 'Two grannies – how will we stick it at all!'

'We've no room here for evacuees,' they said. 'We've only a small house; we'll get you a cup of tea now but you can't stay.'

My mother was nervous but we were all looking at her and she said, 'You're my aunts. We're not evacuees.'

They surveyed us all and then one said, 'God help us all. You're Patrick's daughter. And the grandchildren. And are you bombed out?'

My mother told them no except for the windows and ceilings and that we could go back if there was no room. We had only run away without thinking because we were frightened and that a lot of other people were the same.

They knew about the crowds coming and it seemed to terrify them. It's queer how the thought of Belfast people breaking out away from their backstreets strikes the fear of God into country people. But they wouldn't hear of us going – we'd all fit in grand but it was a small place and we mustn't expect too much.

three

The kitchen was dark after the bright sun on the whitewashed walls outside. There was a table covered with red and white oil-cloth under a small square window. Half of one wall was taken up by an open fire just glowing and a big griddle hanging over it on an iron cleek with farls of bread propped up on their ends smelling of fresh sodas and scorching flour. A black kettle stood on the hob. There was a wall at right-angles to the fireplace and a bench along it. We sat down there and my mother was put in a chair and the aunts fussed about making us tea and boiling us eggs. We ate a lot of their bread hot with the yellow salty butter melting into it but we didn't like the tea because it was strong with sugar and big splashes of milk in it. My mother said we didn't take sugar but they said, 'Of course ye do. Such blathers,' and put another spoonful in each cup. They didn't take any tea with us because I could see they had only four cups.

After a while one asked, 'How did you find your way here?' and my mother told them she remembered her father bringing them to visit many a time while they were children, and even though they came on the train then, she knew exactly where the house was. They looked at each other with such delight that I felt the same as when Mary Brigid and I hug each other. They were both fat; but Maggie was just a fat woman, while Bessie was enormous; not tall either of them and their faces no more than plump but from the chin down they went out and out all round.

'Your mother never bothered with us here at all,' Maggie said in a kind of question. 'My mother was a townswoman,' Mammy said, 'she thought the country was a dangerous place,' and she laughed a wee bit. 'She died just before the war started.' They looked at each other again and nodded. 'We thought that must be her death in the paper,' Maggie said, 'but we weren't sure and we had no way of getting up to Belfast to the funeral.'

I thought my mother would go sad but they all started talking about beds and Danny was sent down with a note to a house that was pointed out to him from the door to ask could they borrow a camp bed for him. He came back to say they could have it and welcome but to wait and send for it after dark so that nobody would know their business. So Danny slept in front of the kitchen fire and the two big fat aunts got into a small double bed in the front bedroom off the kitchen and my mother, Mary Brigid and I slept in the back bedroom. Mary Brigid and my mother slept at the top of the bed and I had a pillow at the bottom with my feet up beside my mother's face. The bed sagged in the middle – up top and bottom and at the two sides – so it wasn't easy to settle even though we were so tired.

My mother covered my feet with her two hands and began to rub the soles of them with her thumbs. Then she said, 'Martha, love, your feet. They're all corns!' I told her I knew that but it didn't matter. They did hurt a bit as if I had little stones in my shoes but I didn't tell her that – I knew it was from standing in the mill. A great many of the girls went in their bare feet but I was always a bit prim, maybe. Anyway I wouldn't bring myself to go barefoot or to link arms with other girls at home-time and spread out across the pavement.

'You're not going back to that mill,' my mother said, 'stay here and get the colour back in your cheeks.'

'Ach, Mammy don't be daft. Of course I'm going back,' I laughed but then she said, 'What would your father say if I didn't look after you right?' and it was as if she pushed me away because I thought then that she didn't love me herself but only had to do her duty to my father. I'm sure it was a silly thing to think but I felt a real pain and I have often thought that parents should be very careful what they say to their children for fear of hurting them. In the morning she said she was going home but could we stay for a wee while in safety and the aunts said yes although I could see they were a bit nervous. I took my courage in my hands and said, 'You'll be lonely, Mammy, in the house by yourself.' As if she wasn't thinking at all, she said, 'I've never been alone in my life. It'll be a nice change for me.' She went back on the evening bus.

That next week was terrible. I began to think I was more like my grandmother than I liked because I found the country threatening – the big open sky, the silences and the feeling of being abandoned. I was afraid of the goat, the geese, the cows, the dogs – even the hens in the henhouse, the way they fluttered and squawked when I opened the door. The cuckoo wakened me every morning in the first light and it cuckooed all day and every day till I wondered why anyone was ever excited at hearing it. For breakfast we were given porridge with goat's milk on it. I didn't like it. I wasn't used to porridge and I hated the texture of it but the goat's milk really poisoned it. I ate it because I would not offend the aunts for all the world. They had no obligation to us and they had little money and we were putting them out. But Mary Brigid didn't feel like that. All she was thinking about was getting back to Belfast, to her school as soon as it opened and to her friends whom I had never met. So she wouldn't eat her breakfast and to keep things pleasant I'd eat hers as well as my own when the aunts weren't looking. Then I'd feel sick for a couple of hours afterwards and she would enjoy eating the lovely bread. I tried to get Danny to eat the extra porridge because his appetite was an embarrassment to me, but he wouldn't.

He didn't behave well at all. He disgraced us. He threw a dead fish into the rainwater barrel and when Maggie ordered him to take it out at once he laughed and ran away leaving me to grope for ages to find the slithery soft thing at the bottom of the water. I carried it on a big heavy spade and buried it in a corner of the garden. He also shot a hen. It was an old hen that had stopped laying and Bessie had said that when the hen-man called on Friday they'd sell it to him. Danny had made friends with a boy who had an airgun and they took it into the field, put pellets into it and Danny shot the hen straight through the eye while it was walking about and Danny was twenty yards away.

It didn't die but ran round and round clucking and squawking. It would have broken your heart.

'It'll drop dead any minute,' Danny said, 'that's just reflex action,' but it didn't and I had to run and beg Maggie to please, please come and do something. She panted up the lane and caught it and wrung its neck. She told the other boy to take himself and his gun out of her field but she didn't say anything to Danny and he was just grinning, not a bit abashed.

I borrowed a stamp and wrote to my mother telling her we'd have to be brought home. She arrived on Sunday on a lorry that came out from Belfast to take back all the people who couldn't stand any more of the country. There had been no air raids in the meantime so they thought the war was finished as far as Belfast was concerned. I felt such relief at seeing her that my legs trembled. But she had decided Mary Brigid couldn't afford to miss school and Danny was too unbiddable to be away from home but if the aunts could find room for me to stay a wee while longer it would do me all the good in the world and I could maybe be useful to them around the house. I couldn't believe it. My mother never asked anybody for anything and here she was imposing me on their poverty. They assured her they would be delighted to keep me and they discussed what to do about my ration book and sweetie coupons and so on but they would take no money from my mother. They told her I would be worth my weight in gold.

The lorry went off up the little narrow road with people all singing and happy at going back to Belfast and my mother holding on tight to Mary Brigid and Danny and I turned back into the dark kitchen thinking if I could go to bed early I could cry into the pillow. But the aunts had decided that each of them should have her own bedroom again and I could sleep on the camp bed in the kitchen. They gave me an old tea-chest covered in wallpaper with big pink roses on it to keep my belongings in. It was well I didn't have much.

four

I have always hoped they didn't see how miserable I was but they must have had an inkling for they kept me very busy. It was then that Bessie taught me to make soda bread. She was not a good teacher because she didn't really know how she did it herself.

'You put in a lock of flour and a taste of salt and baking soda and just the right amount of buttermilk and there you are.' The first couple of times watching I was lost and then decided we'd do it properly. When she poured flour into the big delft bowl with the yellowish outside I poured it out again on a newspaper and measured it in cupfuls so that I would know how much again and I worked out that it was a flat teaspoon of soda and a heaped one of salt and I made her put the buttermilk in a can and marked the can. At first she thought I must be stupid because she never remembered a time when she didn't bake but she said if that way suited me to go ahead. When I baked my first griddleful and it was slightly inferior to hers (a bit tougher) she was really pleased and praised me to the skies.

Maggie showed me how to weed the lettuces and scallions and to sell them to anyone who came looking for them. She charged a penny each for the scallions and I was a bit shocked because that was far dearer than in town. She thought I would like to feed the hens but when she saw how scared I was of them she laughed a bit and said she'd let me off till I got sense. I was ready to do jobs for them and messages but I had one outstanding horror and that was that they'd ask me to empty the outside toilet. It was in the farthest shed from the house. First of all there was a big open shed with an old tipped-up trap in it, a little shed for the goat, a medium one for the hens and then the toilet with a door that didn't properly cover the opening and the road ran just past it, although there was a hedge with an overgrown elder bush in between. I never got used to it. God knows we weren't pampered at home with the toilet at the end of the yard but at least it was private and solid and it flushed. In the daytime in this I felt exposed to the whole countryside and at night with the scufflings and flutterings of the hens and the bushes I was sure there were rats ready to charge in at me. They kept it as nicely as possible but what would I do if they asked me to empty it. I'd get sick. I would have to get away before that happened.

What did happen was the May blitz on Belfast on a Sunday night. I was nearly asleep when I heard the first big crump. I sat up to listen and the camp bed creaked and I told myself it was only my own heart that was thumping. Soon there was no mistaking the sound of bombs only I had to find out where they were. I had still to get my bearings in that place but the mountains on the far side of the lough were where the sun set so I knew Belfast was opposite that. I put on my coat and my shoes and I could see people out and lights on in houses. There were no hills near us but I went up the road a bit and the sound seemed to echo all around. Then I saw red in the sky from fires and I asked a man on the road was that over Belfast. They talked very slowly there and he looked at me and said, 'Why?' in a long drawn-out way. I told him I was from Belfast and he said, 'Well, it's in that general direction. But it might be Lisburn now or some other place along the road. They're all out there.' He was a bad liar and I started to shiver and shake so that I had to sit down on the bank at the side of the road. I could hear them talking about me. One man arrived shouting, 'D'ye see that? Belfast's a bombin'!' and the others shushed him and I heard them mention Bessie and Maggie Lavery.

I was afraid they would be disturbed so I went back to their house and sat on the seat inside the jamb wall crying about my mother and Mary Brigid and even Danny. My main worry, although I didn't really admit it to myself, was that if anything happened to my mother I would have nobody to rescue me from the country and nobody to get me a job or money again. Then I began to be glad I wasn't in that noise and terror, that I was here alive in a cool country night and not in any danger, so I cried some more to hide that from myself because I was ashamed. In the small hours the bombing stopped and I got into bed. I had heard the aunts' beds groaning and I thought they were likely awake but we didn't know one another well enough at that stage to be any help.

I always got up early for fear somebody would come to the door so I was dressed when a man knocked and said he was taking a lorry to Belfast and if I would tell him my mother's address he'd call on them and see did they want out. They were kind people, kind good people. He brought me a letter that night from my mother to say they were safe, the bombing was down town, buildings that had nothing to do with our life. She was glad I was safe out in the quiet, able to get my sleep and good food and I was to be as helpful as possible to the aunts and no bother to anybody.

I had no money – not a ha'penny. I was used to that but I was used also to having all my needs provided for by my mother. I asked the aunts was there any kind of work around about – there were no factories, no shops that weren't run by the owners. They told me some girls made a little money hemming wee linen handkerchiefs. So I tried that but I was very slow and I'd clutch them too tight and crumple them. Then they asked me would I think it beneath me to spring-clean a lady-teacher's house up on the main road. I didn't think it beneath me but at home what had we to clean! We washed the floors and the yard and kept the rest wiped down. What did I know about spring-cleaning?

The teacher, Miss Rankin, lived in a cottage not unlike the aunts' except that she had a 'room', and that was what I was to clean. I arrived at nine o'clock expecting her to be on her way out but she hovered about showing me dusters and brushes and polishes half a dozen times. 'That'll do for the furniture polish – it's nice and soft. No, still there's a better one there. Or maybe this one if it hasn't too much fluff on it.' She had a whole bag of cloths. 'That would do then for the Brasso. Just burn it when you've done with it – it'll be black. Oh no, maybe leave it for me to burn – you don't want to blaze up the fire and light the thatch. Will you be able to make yourself a cup of tea at twelve o'clock? Or would you rather go home and come back? I'd give you the key if I could find it.' Then there was a hunt for the key. 'It's not that anybody would steal anything, but those McQuillans across the road, they'd come in just to have a look round.' She found the key in her bag and then said maybe she should make me a cup of tea herself. I said no I could manage but she'd be very late for school – at this time it was nearly ten o'clock. She looked surprised. 'Oh, not at all. Sure with double summer time it's not eight yet, and then with twenty-five minutes between our time and London time it's just after half past seven. The poor children are hardly out of their beds.' She seemed as mad as Miss Killeen in Belfast but not in the same way, not at all in the same way.

When she was gone eventually I surveyed the room. It was crammed. There was a carpet on the floor that I could hardly see with all the furniture on it. There was an old black piano with red silk bits on the front of it and brass candle-holders to pull forward or fold back as you wanted. There was a round mahogany table with a dark green chenille cover trimmed with baubles, and chairs round it, and then two big armchairs at the fireplace, and against the wall on either side two bookcases with glass doors on top and green puckered cloth behind the glass so that I couldn't see the books. I never saw so many pictures, all higgledy-piggledy – brown pictures of cows and longhorns in mist and water, grey pictures of cavaliers, a picture of a very sweetly smiling old-fashioned boy and girl with a basket of wild strawberries between them, and underneath was written, 'If you love me as I love you nothing will ever part us two.' Over the mantelpiece was a mirror with grey speckled glass and reflected in it from above the piano was a picture of a beautiful dark-haired, brown-eyed woman, so dignified and grave. I kept on looking at her. The teacher told me afterwards it was a photo-graph taken long ago and then handpainted, her cheeks pink, her dress dark blue and a big feathery fan in her hand a sort of turquoise colour. I never knew who it was. When I asked was it her mother she just said no, in surprise as if I should know all about her. I wondered if her mother was dead, and if she was as lonely for her as I was for mine.

I thought I would wash the curtains first but when I took them down off the two windows I saw they were in ribbons, every fold rotted with dust or sun or damp. So I hung them on the line to air and watched that the nice fresh breeze didn't blow them to bits every time it lifted them up in a billow. I lugged the chairs out to her front yard and battered the dust out of them, clouds of it out of the red plush seats, and then polished up the carved wooden parts. I couldn't put them back until I had all inside cleared. I had a big witch's broom to sweep with and the aunts had saved tea-leaves for me to scatter on the floor beforehand to keep down the dust.

I didn't stop for anything to eat. I didn't ease up even for a minute. I had a kind of a hectic feeling that I wouldn't be done or nearly done when she came home from school. I didn't know what way she had for reckoning the clock in the evening. And sure enough I was polishing the brass candle-holders when I heard her car turning into the yard and then such fuss. She came in carrying a big armchair all out of breath for she was a frail thin bit of a woman.

'Get all those chairs in this instant. Are you trying to disgrace me? The whole country'll be talking. Come on. Help me. Come on. In with them. Quick. Oh, the McQuillans will have a field-day!' She was so upset I just hurried to do what she said and I was glad the place was ready for them. Then when she was beginning to subside and putting her two hands up to her neck to hold herself together she caught sight of the curtains on the line and the hands flew out again and away she was, pulling them in. I was afraid they'd disintegrate before I'd get them up again – they went on a kind of a spiral stretchy wire with a ring at either end to hook it across the window and a frill on top. 'I need new curtains,' she said, 'I must buy cloth. It's not the

40

money, you know, it's the coupons,' and I thought the same curtains were worn out before the war started.

When she had time to look round she told me I had made everything very nice and she'd send word when she wanted me again. I said I was sorry about the chairs outside but I told her she had lovely furniture and if anybody took any notice it would be to think how well-off she was with cushioned chairs when the rest of us had only wooden ones we could scrub. She said I couldn't know about the country, that it was different in town. I thought to myself it surely was. But she gave me five shillings and offered to lend me a bicycle to go home on since I lived 'away down the Moss'. Only I had to tell her I couldn't ride a bicycle and she was amazed and told me to learn as soon as possible.

What could I learn on? I trudged miles along those little narrow roads, it took so long to get places. The aunts had a dressmaker away along the lough road. I used to walk there to find out if she really had the dresses ready for fitting before the aunts got a ride in a trap or cart to her house. Hardly anybody had cars on the road and people who were allowed petrol coupons couldn't waste them. The trips ended so often in excuses and disappointment and a long walk home with the sun on my back, that I made up my mind to get a bicycle somehow. There were two old frames in a shed in the aunts' field and they said they would ask around for wheels. But the next time I went to Miss Rankin's house to scrub down her kitchen she told me to take her bicycle out on the station road and learn to ride it. I was delighted with myself when I could balance it and I'd have ridden miles straight away only the pedal kept coming off and men passing by kept asking me if I had engine trouble while I was shoving it on. When I was going home after the cleaning was done she told me to take the bicycle, that it was for me. When I stuttered and stammered she said sort of absent-mindedly that she had two bicycles and didn't need that old one. Sure enough I saw her on a different one a couple of weeks later but it was a new utility one that you could buy for three pounds if you were

41

well in with the bicycle shop owner – he was allocated only a few in the year.

I didn't know myself, sitting up sedately spinning along after Maggie got a man to fix the pedal. One thing I hated about walking was meeting people. I know they would say hello or give me that slow sideways nod the men used, but I could see them so far ahead that I'd grow so awkward before they'd pass that I wouldn't know where to look. On the bicycle it was grand. I took to pestering the dressmaker. I'd ride down the stony road between wee swampy fields and then I'd turn on to a slightly bigger road with the lough on one side and bog on the other. I could see the lough only at a few places because between there were thick sally and elder bushes right down to the water's edge, and hanging out over it with swirls of midges all summer. There was a boy I'd see sometimes on the side of the road just past the little two-teacher Moss school, a big red-headed boy sitting on the bank knitting a red jersey that clashed with his hair. I nearly fell off my bike with astonishment the first time I saw him and he laughed and shouted, 'Hello, wee Townie,' after me. Bessie told me there was nothing strange about it. The old teacher in that school was useless except at knitting and she taught boys and girls alike to knit because it kept them out of mischief at school. Some of them carried it on afterwards if they didn't mind their families and friends jeering at them.

The dressmaker was no good. When eventually she produced the dresses they didn't even fit. The waists were too high. So now I had money for paper and a stamp, I wrote to my mother. I suggested that if she could somehow get a good many yards of cloth it would be nice for her to make for the aunts. She came out the next Sunday – it cost her two shillings and eleven pence return by bus, and she brought a summer dress for me and her tape measure for the aunts, and some sugar for them because the country people used so much more than we did in Belfast. I never heard such laughing from grown-ups as when they were being measured. I think my mother was afraid they would be embarrassed at being so fat but when the tape was put round

Maggie's bust, waist and hips Bessie laughed like a tickled toddler and when it was Bessie's turn Maggie had to sit down in the armchair for laughing and leaned back with her two feet on her little short legs lifted off the ground. Then we had our tea and my mother was smiling and eating plenty of bread. She said it was no wonder I had such a good colour and my hair was looking so well. The aunts said it was the rainwater I was always washing it with but there was more to it than that. When my mother used to try to fix it nicely my granny used to say, 'Sure she has only wee wisps of hair,' and I'd pray at night that I'd waken up with masses of curls. In the country it did thicken, maybe from the fresh air, maybe from all the vegetables we ate. We had meat once a week. The butcher called in a van and cut it for his customers on a block in the back.

He also brought the *Irish Weekly*, our only contact with the world. Some people had radios and saved them for the news – I would hear them fussing about wet batteries and dry batteries. They listened to the BBC and said why couldn't they talk ordinary like us and anyway it was all propaganda. They listened to Lord Haw-Haw and believed him, not only in what he said had happened but in what they were told he had said would happen. I heard him a few times in other people's houses but never saying anything of interest although that cold deep voice of his made me shiver. They were always saying he talked about Ireland. On one of my trips to the dressmaker when I went along to the Featherbed road to pull wild raspberries I heard an old woman shouting to a man at a distance, 'Lord Haw-Haw says the border's to go.' I couldn't catch his answer but she said, 'Oh he's the boy knows what's to happen. If he says it'll go then it'll go.' She had a man's panama hat on because the sun was hot and she was cutting turf, poor scraws of stuff that blazed up in a minute and was gone with no heat. But coal was scarce and dear and there were no trees to get wood from in the Moss.

I was glad the people there too cared about a united Ireland. I had heard the priest pray at Mass each Sunday for a couple of names 'who had been interned during the week' and I thought how kind of him since nobody in Belfast proposed praying for them. I prayed for my father although he was a distant figure by then, vague with no weight. I asked the aunts one Sunday, 'Are there many IRA men round about?' They were startled, the way people are all over when such a question is asked. 'A few maybe,' Maggie answered. 'At the lough shore over near the dressmaker's.'

'There were two lifted this week,' I said and they both turned on me. 'Who were you talking to? Where did you hear that?' They laughed and laughed, they were so relieved, when I told them about the priest and of course they explained the word was 'interred' and the priest was old-fashioned using a big word instead of buried. I couldn't help crying a wee bit then. I don't know why I was sad but I told them about my father even though I could see they knew the main facts. My mother said afterwards she'd never mentioned my father to them because the opportunity didn't come up, but people in the country know all there is to be known about one another.

I kept on going to clean the teacher's house every week even when she was at home during the summer holidays. Sometimes she went off straight away on her bike or in her car – it was a black Ford people said cost a hundred pounds. Sometimes she pottered about the house and I tried not to get in her way. I'd polish the piano or crawl round the room dusting the claw feet on tables and chairs. If she stayed in the room with me she talked in an absent-minded way as if she wasn't a bit interested in me but one day she opened the bookcase and asked me did I ever read at all. 'I have no books,' I said, 'I used to have books my father bought but they're all in Belfast. Nobody much in the country seems to have books.' She asked me my age and when I told her fifteen she said she didn't think she had much I'd like, except Dickens and Scott. Her father, God rest him, she said, used to read Dickens one winter and Scott the next and nothing but the newspaper in the summer. 'You might like this,' she said, and she handed me a book called *Coming Through the Rye* and told me to take it home and read it. I thought it was the loveliest book. When I was ten we did *Little Women* at school and I read it over and over, always going off to the toilet to cry when I knew the sad parts were coming. This book had a bit of the same flavour. I never saw it anywhere else but Miss Rankin had it in Irish too. She had about a dozen Irish books. She asked me did I know Irish but I had learnt only the Our Father and Hail Mary in Irish. She said she was always going to learn and maybe she would when she retired only she didn't know who would take on to teach the teacher. She'd laugh now and again when she was talking like that. She told me about the county library in a woman's house a couple of miles away, supplied by a van that changed the books. She told me she had to let you in for a book if you asked but that she tried not to let people know because she didn't want people coming into her house.

It was a house in the square where the bus for Lurgan sat in the hot sun. The walls were cut black stone, with windows shining like diamonds. The woman herself was stout and stiff with a wool jumper stretched over a bust that had no division. She made all kinds of difficulties while keeping me standing on the metal shoe-scraper outside the door. I'd need to get a ticket and when I said all right I knew about library tickets and could I have a form please, she didn't know had she any forms and anyway I'd need a guarantor who was a householder. The aunts owned their house and four acres so that was no difficulty but the whole delaying carry-on made me impatient and I said to the aunts that I supposed she was a Protestant. They didn't approve of that. Maggie said, 'Well of course she's a Protestant with a name like Anderson and she wouldn't get the library if she wasn't, but there's nothing wrong with Protestants here you know. They're fine decent people and good neighbours.' I was cross with them for checking me and I said, 'I don't see many of them living near here as neighbours.' 'Well, no,' they said, 'the land here wouldn't be good enough for them. But there's nothing to stop a hard-working Catholic farmer buying one of the good farms on higher ground if the Protestant family dies out and it's put up for sale.' They mentioned somebody buying a house called Prosperous and paying off the whole price of the farm with the money he got for the Bramley apple crop the next autumn because of no apple imports during the war.

When I persevered about the library tickets I got into the blackstone house after being told several times to be sure and wipe my feet – there was a succession of mats. The library books were in a glass-fronted bookcase as if they were her own. The books were mostly new, printed in wartime on yellowish paper and covered badly. My recollection of them is that they were all about village life in England during the war. They were like reading fairy stories, everything was in such order. There was the big house, the vicarage, the church, the doctor and the villagers. They all worked together in such unity I could only laugh. And of course they were every one Protestants. Until I was grown up I never came across any book that mentioned Catholics. In spite of learning in the catechism that the Church was universal I felt always that Catholics were only fit for backstreets and boglands and if by any chance you penetrated into the Protestant world they would no more mention your strange religion than they would draw attention to a disfiguring birthmark. I didn't think we were inferior except in wealth and opportunity but to the world I glimpsed in books we were invisible.

I read lying out on a sunny bank at the top of the aunts' big field or sometimes in a wee clump of trees I found with a stream running over white stones and a silver birch beside it. It wasn't as comfortable there as on the grassy bank and being shady was not as warm but I thought it was romantic and maybe as good as Mary Brigid's tree growing outside her schoolroom window. So when I had my books and my cleaning money and my bicycle and the two summer dresses my mother had made me I began to write letters to Mary Brigid to tell her what it was really like and to tempt her to come and squash into my camp bed during the summer holidays. She never came to stay. She'd come the odd Sunday with my mother but she said she couldn't risk the porridge and goat's milk even though I told her over and over that we never had that for ourselves. The aunts didn't coax her to come. I think they thought she was cheeky. All she was interested in was her school – and her schoolfriends. She wrote pages of letters. The aunts called them bibles, they were so long to read. They went on about people I didn't know any more than I knew the English people in the library books.

When the days drew in and the apples in all the orchards ripened I got no more opportunity to read. I was the opposite of Miss Rankin's father. I had no place to read in the house. There was an oil lamp nailed to the wall with a bright tin reflector but the light didn't come down to the pages of a book. And people came to visit, oldish people. It would have been bad manners if I hadn't listened even though they sat close round the fire and I stayed back where the draughts made my feet and hands numb. The door had to be left open to the yard or the fire smoked. I wished that I had some place to go, another room or another house. I didn't know anybody well enough that winter to go to the socials and dances that were held in the local halls. I often felt I was a blight on the visits because the aunts would allow no scandal while I was there. They would clip it short with a jerk of their heads towards me, and the conversation would fall into one of the usual ruts – dirt, rats, prices or cookery. It wasn't always women who came in although they were commonest. The hen-man, who lived with his two sisters whose camp bed I still used, came regularly. He never wanted to go home. Bessie told me laughing how they used to say to him, 'Goodnight now, John Francis, we're off to bed. Just turn out the lamp and see the fire is safe before you go.' And he wouldn't move for more than an hour. But with me there they couldn't do that and we all had to sit up late yawning.

Why didn't I go home to Belfast? There were all kinds of reasons – fear of another blitz, reluctance to go back to the mill, a wee bit of satisfaction in independence. But mostly it was resentment nursed and nourished against my mother and Mary Brigid for having their own full lives and being able to do without me. I loved them and when either of them was with me I was happy and relaxed but at night I'd say to myself that they had no time for me or they'd ask me to come home, and that I'd never go until they begged me no matter how homesick I was. And my father? He was a figure from my childhood of kindness, love, security, but I didn't hanker for him any more than I wanted to go back to my childhood. My mother went to see him, but only my mother, and his messages to me were filtered through her. Sometimes I wondered did he remember me at all or did my mother invent messages so that I wouldn't be offended. The things he was supposed to have said had no special flavour of him. Other times I thought she suppressed what he had said because she was jealous of how much he had loved me as a wee girl. I could have written him letters, but I didn't, and he didn't write to me. They would have been read and censored by the gaol authorities but why should that have worried me?

The only one I really wrote to was Mary Brigid except for notes to my mother about arrangements of some sort for her visits or clothes she was making for me or the aunts. I was an encumbrance to the aunts but I think maybe I was useful and maybe when they were accustomed to me ready to hop up on the bicycle and ride off on errands or weed the garden or scrub the kitchen they would have missed me had I left. We were friendly but not affectionate. They loved each other, that was enough for them at their time of life. I used to wonder had they ever thought of getting married before they grew so fat. Had they ever dreamed of having someone to love, some man who would wrap his arms round them and smile at them and admire them and laugh with them. They weren't bad-looking and they knew everybody. They tried to explain to me the relationships for generations back in their own family and in any other family ever mentioned spread all over the Moss. I didn't follow it. It seemed pointless to me.

five

I didn't see much of the big red-headed boy that winter, or of any other young people. I went up to the teacher's house to clean, I went to the next village to the library; but neither of these roads went near where I'd seen him in the summer. Anyway, nobody was sitting on ditches while the little streams of water running all over the roads were frozen white morning and evening, or while big drifts of rain swept over from the mountains on the far side of the lough. Sometimes the clouds seemed to point down into the shiny expanse of water and people said, 'Streamers to the lough. It'll rain before dark.' They told me the clouds sucked up the water. I laughed to myself at them even though it generally did rain.

I never laughed out loud at them since the first autumn. I was on the yard wall pulling bunches of elderberries for Maggie and reaching them down to where she was holding them in a tin basin when one of the Thompson brothers stopped on the road to talk to her. Their fields were on much better land but sometimes when they had brought new bullocks from the mid-lands they used fields near ours. Big heavy cattle they were with white faces and horns. They were left there for a while and then sold to England. The brothers were both bachelors. They lived in a smallish house without much comfort and with a barking dog chained up at the gate. I was always afraid riding past their house that the stretched chain would suddenly break and the dog come tearing after me. It was said they had fortunes in pound notes in the house for buying and selling bullocks. That day Andrew was admiring the sheen of the September sun on the lough and he said, 'Isn't it a funny thing, Maggie – you see the lough here and you turn your back on it and you keep going with your back to it and still when you arrive in Belfast and go down to the boat there is the lough in front of you!' I started to laugh and I was all for enlightening him from my great geography

49

learning that it was a different lough but I got a very sharp look from Maggie and I shut my mouth and busied myself at the elderberries. 'I don't go to Belfast myself,' was all Maggie said to him but when he was well away she scolded me, 'Andrew may not know much out of books, Martha – Protestants don't have the same regard for education as we have because they have so much else. Half time they have no teacher at all in their national school at "the corners" and other times it's only a wee ignorant girl. But Andrew and William can go to Mullingar and back and know every step of the way. You're a smart girl, Martha, anybody can see that, but there's people know things not in brains or books.' I was very chastened.

That winter America came into the war and American soldiers began to appear in the countryside. We heard of them before we saw them. A couple of them, drunk, beat a publican to death because he wouldn't open his pub for them after hours. 'Savages,' everybody said. And then these big tall men in pinkish-beige trousers and beautifully tailored jackets were seen slouching around Lurgan, chewing gum and looking unhappy. We surveyed them. 'They never had shoes on their feet until they were put into uniform,' was the general explanation for their unfamiliar walk. 'They come from the back of beyond in America. They don't talk a bit like the pictures.' Nice girls did not speak to them. There was a tale that in the Methodist chapel communicants would not touch the chalice after a girl who had been 'with Americans'.

English soldiers we had seen since the beginning of the war – their lorries went in convoys along the narrow roads. They whistled at girls and you could either smile a bit or ignore them depending on how much on your dignity you felt. Generally speaking it must be admitted they behaved like gentlemen. They wore hairy khaki and big hard boots that struck sparks out of the road and when they had to live rough on manoeuvres they had a can for drinking out of and an oblong tin with a fold-up handle to heat their food in. They asked permission to use the pump and they apologised for blocking yards or gates. Such a difference between then and now. They were conscripts. We didn't have conscription although the Unionists were loud in their demands for it but only one of the well-to-do Protestant young men in my part of the country joined up during the war. His father came to our door to collect money for 'the Russian war effort'. Bessie didn't ask him in. 'I have no money for the Russians, Mr Walker,' she said, 'there's plenty nearer home have more need. How about helping out people like this wee girl whose father is interned this time just because he was interned the last time. Start a fund like that, now, and I'd save up for it.' He was all embarrassed and indeed so was I and we were sorry afterwards when his son came back in a wheelchair. In Belfast a whole lot of poor Catholic boys went into the army because they had no work and anyway they were ready for adventure.

But the Americans had endless money. There was a big rush job to build an airport for the heavy planes that brought in the soldiers and the jeeps and the flour and the butter and the sweets and each little thing they needed for every day in their lives. Every able-bodied man and boy from miles around seemed to be working on that airport down at the lough shore. They were able then to buy new trousers instead of going round in patched threadbare old suits, or new shoes for evenings instead of smelly rubber boots all the time. They stood at the usual places on the roads in the long spring evenings and summer Sundays, far more full of themselves.

By that time I was seventeen and friends with a girl of my own age, Rachel Reid, who lived with her grandfather down at the corners. She worked in an office in Lisburn and went off on the eight o'clock bus in the mornings and came back at half-seven every evening. Still she was ready to fly off on her bicycle and call for me. She was a lovely looking girl with golden-brown hair and skin the colour of apricot silk, much bigger than me and more noticeable but the big red-headed boy singled me out. He was called Hugh Mulholland but I never got the length of calling him anything – I was too shy, not to talk to him but to use his name. He called me 'Wee Townie' most of the time. When he called me Martha I knew he was beginning to be serious about me.

The boys used to circle on their bikes or tear up the road and back again. The girls stood in clumps or sat on the bank if it wasn't wet. It was very much as I've watched blackbirds in the spring only we were not so single-minded about what we wanted. We were happy enough with the little extra excitement it gave us – at least I was. I used to lie in bed at night smiling to myself and making up grand conversations that never emerged. I am certain sure that if all commandments and embargoes had been removed and we were free to behave the way we are told young people do now, we'd all have headed for home as quick as our coggledy bikes would carry us. Maybe I'm wrong. Maybe the others were not like me. Hugh was not good-looking, none of the boys were. Generally the people of the Moss were short and broad. But he was always laughing and he rode his bike faster than anybody else and pulled it up sharper so that the tyres squealed. When the lough froze in a very cold winter towards the end of the war he rode his bicycle over the ice to Ram's Island and back. Most of the boys contented themselves with throwing stones and half bricks to litter the thick ice. Standing around to watch I thought I would die of the cold. I have no spirit of adventure.

I knew he had two sisters in the sanatorium with TB. I knew his elder brother had died vomiting blood in the house before they even found out he was sick but I didn't see that these things were any business of mine any more than the fact that my father was in gaol would trouble him. There were no secrets in the country although some people were worried more about their neighbours knowing things than about the things themselves. Still it was nearly the end of the war before my aunts spoke to me about Hugh Mulholland. In all that time we never actually went out together. We met in groups or we went to the dances. I didn't like the dust and the noise but he was mad about dancing. We might talk at the side of the road but weeks would go by in bad weather when we wouldn't see each other at all. Then I'd be wishing my life away waiting for the next time I'd see his face break into a smile when he'd look at me. One of his sisters died and I saw him crying at the funeral, holding on to his wee brother's hand and not even wiping away the tears.

'We have to talk to you, Martha,' Maggie said when I was cutting up apples to make apple slim. They made it on the griddle, pastry top and bottom and apples, sugar and a few cloves in the middle, like apple tart without the plate. They were both there – Bessie rolling out the pastry and Maggie fixing the fire so that it would have just the right glow.

'People say that you're seeing a lot of Hugh Mulholland,' Maggie said and my face went red and I was tempted to deny it but instead I looked at their accusing faces.

I said, 'What's the harm in that? I'm eighteen, he's nineteen. We're not thinking of getting married or anything. You don't have to ask him his intentions!' I tried to make a joke of it but they were serious.

'Don't you know the whole family is riddled with T B?' Maggie said. 'Generation after generation in that wee house. The walls are full of it.'

'I'm never in the house,' I said.

'That doesn't matter,' Maggie said. 'Just being with him is enough to give you the germ. Supposing he coughed when you weren't in the best of form, where would you be? Spitting up blood in a week or two. Don't laugh now! It's no laughing matter. If Miss Rankin got to hear that you were going with Hugh Mulholland she wouldn't let you inside her door, much less touch her dishes and food. And the farmhouses you go to at haymaking and threshing would have a good excuse to keep you well away from them. Your library books too – they'd be taken away from you.'

'There's nothing wrong with Hugh Mulholland,' I said. 'He's not sick. He hasn't got a cough.'

'It's only a matter of time,' Bessie said. She was always softer than Maggie. 'It's a sad thing to see a family like that dying one after the other while the mother and father are still alive even though they're not strong. It's unnatural but that's the way consumption works. You just have to keep away from it. What would your mother say if you lost your health and strength while we were responsible for you?'

It was no wonder I had a hankering to have Hugh Mulholland love me because none of my family would admit they loved me at all. The aunts were only minding me for my mother, my mother for my father, and my father didn't know me, couldn't know me. If he remembered me at all it was as a wee girl of thirteen. He didn't know how capable I was, how the aunts could depend on me, and Miss Rankin and anybody else who needed help in the kitchen. Even the library woman had let me rearrange new books now and again and she didn't stand behind me any more while I was looking through her bookcase. I was in charge of my own life and if I chose to meet Hugh Mulholland nobody had the right to stop me.

So, in a way, I went on seeing him but the winter was coming in and there were not so many chances and I found myself listening would he cough, and not able to meet his eyes when he'd smile at me. When I'd be cycling home cold, I'd remember the sun on my back in early July on the Featherbed road and the smell of raspberries as I pulled them into a tin can and it would strike me that if I got TB I might die without ever feeling such things again. After the winter was over I wouldn't go out at all with Rachel Reid and she stopped being friends with me. I went to no socials or dances. I stopped to talk to no young people on the road. I wanted to go back to Belfast, just to run away like the coward I was.

six

Then Bessie got sick and stayed in bed. She said she was just too tired to carry herself round any more so she lay there dozing, eating very little no matter what dainty things we cooked for her. Nursing her was a great trouble, she was so heavy and the bed was against the wall. At night when we'd finished our rosary Maggie used to say she didn't know under God what she'd do without me. I did anything that had to be done, washed sheets from poor Bessie's incontinence, carried bedpans if Maggie wasn't just there – even emptied and buried the contents of the outside toilet. She died one hot summer afternoon with a bluebottle buzzing trapped against her bedroom window. She just stopped breathing.

Everybody for miles around came in during the wake and for her Requiem Mass. As well as the usual congregation the wee bare church was filled with broad Protestant men in good navy suits and very polished shoes. My mother and Mary Brigid and Danny came to the funeral. She was buried in a sunny sheltered graveyard full of midges on a bit of raised ground surrounding a ruined church. Two of our neighbours from the Moss watched the soil being shovelled in on the coffin. 'It's good soil here all the same,' one said to the other. 'D'ye see the nice dry looseness of it, not all clammy like ours.'

'Aye, you could grow something right on that soil,' said the other. 'It's like on George's Island. Did you ever see the blackberries on George's Island? The best blackberries in Ireland! Huge!' Then I noticed Mary Brigid and Danny standing behind them giggling, and I was so annoyed that they were together laughing while I was stuck with the people they were laughing at, and no way to get out of it now unless I left Maggie on her own.

That night Maggie told me she was going into Lurgan in a day or two to make a new will because Bessie and she had each left all to the other but now Maggie was going to leave the place to me. I was in a state – I didn't want to be tied there. 'Oh no, you can't,' I told her. 'I couldn't run your farm. I'm only a townie,' and then I started to cry because of Hugh, and Maggie thought I was sad about Bessie and told me she was gone to her reward and was far better off.

'I don't want you to stay here, Martha,' she told me. 'It's no life for any girl, God knows. Bessie and me had talked it over and we thought when we're both gone you could sell the house and fields. Mind you, you wouldn't get much. You'd not be rich, but you might get a couple of hundred and you could keep it in the bank until you needed it. I'd die happy after Bessie if I thought we had given you a wee nest egg just to keep for yourself. Don't tell anybody you have it, not your mother or that brother and sister of yours or your husband when you get one. Keep it until some day when you need it for something for yourself.'

Of course I protested and said I couldn't take so much, that I owed them instead and I could never hide things from my mother and Mary Brigid. But even while I was saying it I was beginning to think how comfortable it would be to have a bit of money by me.

'You'd wonder what you could do when the time comes,' Maggie said and then she started getting ready for bed. 'Do you want us to fix up Bessie's room for you tomorrow?' she asked me while she was bending over the fire lighting her candle.

I said, 'No, no, not at all,' because Bessie's room smelled to me of death and before that of sickness and before that just of old woman.

The war in Europe was over and Hitler was dead and people began to talk of unemployment again and the Americans going home and not needing their big landing places. Maggie had visitors most nights and nobody was in any great heart. I thought life was dreary and lonely and I couldn't see any way to change it.

Then Maggie cut her ankle on a chipped enamel bucket in the yard and it wouldn't heal. A nasty big gash but she wouldn't get it stitched or go near the doctor until it looked horrible and I asked Miss Rankin if she would be kind enough to drive Maggie up to the doctor's house on the top of the hill. Some of the women loved going to him because he told them they were seriously ill and were 'not to as much as lift a cup'! They paid his fee happily, told all their neighbours and then went on with their usual hard work. Maggie wasn't like that. The only way I could get her to go was to point out what bad manners it would be to Miss Rankin and a waste of her petrol and what a poor light it would put me in.

The doctor said she'd have to go into hospital. I said I could mind her, but the doctor said no there was something wrong with the circulation and it would have to be seen to or she'd get gangrene. She was upset and kept asking how I would manage. I told her I would manage fine except for the goat. I had never dealt with it and I said could I ask the MacNieces down the road to mind it for her. She said I could do anything at all I thought fit and that really I should go back to my mother, but I told her I wouldn't desert her. I'd do her washing and bring her things to the hospital every visiting day.

The first day I went in to see her I couldn't get over the change in her. She looked a picture with her white hair washed and shining. Bessie and she had always scolded me for washing my hair. They said it was bad for it and they would have washed their hair once a year if that. With smoky fires and dirty outhouses it had been greyish yellow.

'Oh, Martha,' she greeted me, 'such a lovely place this is! Why didn't we get Bessie into it so that she could have a bit of luxury before she died? Hot water, electric light, indoor toilets, eating in bed off a tray and nobody to ask me to do a tap! It's just heaven, now that's what it is.' I asked her was her foot sore and she said, 'Ach, well it is, but sure what about that. And do you know I hear women complaining! They're groaning and moaning and ringing for the nurses and saying the beds are hard or the food not good. Some people must have had an easy life if they think there's anything wrong with this.'

Even when they amputated her foot and the skin on her face went into grey folds she was well pleased. 'Martha, don't you see I'll never be out of this. They can't send me home to fend for myself with only one leg. So listen now, you sell the place and go away back to Belfast.' I told her I would do nothing of the sort and recounted all the people who were asking about her and sending her messages and looking forward to her coming home and that I'd be there to look after her. As a matter of fact I wouldn't have had any idea of how to go about selling the place. 'Don't expect me ever to go back there,' she said. 'Heaven must be like this without the foot trouble. Such ease and comfort.'

She died in September 1946 and was buried in her sister's grave, and I went back to Belfast on 16th October 1946. I had lived alone in the wee house for over a year and nobody worried about my safety or well-being. I had to make do on the few shillings a week I earned by cleaning or helping out in farm kitchens and there were times in the winter when I was hungry because work like that wasn't around then. Nobody thought about cleaning the house during the dark days. People gave me presents of bread – 'It's not worth your while baking for one,' they said – and potatoes and wood for the fire and meal for the hens until I sold them off a few at a time to keep going. My mother being a real townswoman thought that in the country food grew on the bushes. It was a bad summer and a worse autumn and from the bus to Belfast I could see fields even on the good land with the stooks of corn still standing, unharvested, and little green shoots growing up round them from the dropped seeds.

seven

The key was in the door when I got home but nobody was in. My mother was still at work, Mary Brigid boarding in the training college where she was learning to be a teacher and Danny, I supposed, had not come home from school with the Christian Brothers where my father's sister in Dublin was paying the fee – three pounds a year it was. She was paying the thirty-five pounds a year for Mary Brigid to live in the college too. I never cost any of them anything.

I stood in the middle of the kitchen floor not knowing whether I was sad or happy to be home. It was not changed one bit over the five years I had been in the country, even the same shiny pink cushion on what used to be Granny's chair. The fire was set but not lit; it was hard to get enough coal to keep a fire going all day if there was nobody in. I looked in the breadbin and found there just one loaf from the shop – a miserable grey thing with a soggy middle like all the rest of the bread available at that time. I thought if I could make a bit of bread in the pan on the gas ring it would heat the room as well as surprise them with the nice smell. But there was no flour, no baking soda, no buttermilk and I had no money and I was tired of looking after myself all alone. I remembered the way my father used to have the place warm and welcoming when I'd come home from school and I began to be horrified at myself that for five and a half years I had not seen him or spoken to him or written to him. I was ashamed that just because he was powerless and useless to me I had nearly forgotten all about him.

The minute my mother came in scolding me for not having lit the fire I demanded to know when my father was being let out. 'Why do they want to keep him so long now that the war's over?'

'They're not keeping him any more. He's not in gaol for nearly a year now. He's in the hospital. He's sick.'

'What's wrong with him?' I asked.

'TB,' she said, just flat, putting a match to the fire.

I burst out laughing. I never understood why but it was much the same as the way I've laughed when I saw dishes dropped and lying broken on the floor. My mother stared at me and her horror stopped me. 'I don't know why you're laughing,' she said, disgusted with me. 'I don't see anything funny in your father lying up there in the freezing cold, all thin and weak and not getting any better even though they've discovered a cure for TB now and other people are getting up and going home, but not Seamus. It doesn't work with him. You're a queer kind of girl, that's all I can say.' I couldn't tell her about having to give up being friends with Hugh Mulholland because of TB in his family so she had no notion what way I was thinking and she didn't like me at all. While I was in the country looking after myself I wished I was being minded by my mother, but that evening eating my tea with my mother and Danny in bad form I thought there was a lot to be said for being alone with nobody to glare at me. Danny just read a book, not even a schoolbook but a trashy paperback about cowboys. He didn't do much schoolwork. He didn't do well with his advantages.

Later that night my mother told me I was not to go back to her mill but to a new factory for making underclothes where they had seats for the girls working. They would pay me less than the mill but the work would be easier. I could see she had arranged it out of kindness and I knew I should get up and hug her or kiss her but I just sat there and said thanks that would be nice.

The factory was a one-storey concrete barn of a place over beside the river that formed the boundary of our parish. It took me a long time to get used to the crowds of girls and the clack of the sewing machines and 'music while you work' coming from the loudspeakers. The slips and pants we made were of smooth hard artificial silk in pink or blue or white or apricot. A whole pile would be cut out at one go by a big blade that followed the pattern. They tried me first as a machinist because that is what my mother entered me for. She was so good with the sewing machine she thought anybody could be, but I was useless – worse than useless. The stitches would either go murderously tight, puckering the material, or else loopy, not catching at all on the wrong side. Nobody else's machine ever got stuck but mine did. They tried me at different machines – machines that had worked perfectly since the factory opened and before the day was over the mechanic would have to come and sort them out – my thread would be bunched up over and around the bobbin. The other women and girls made fun of me in a kindly way to make me laugh, and I did laugh but I hated making a mess of things. I was used to managing fairly well. After a while they changed me to cutting and I was able to do that a bit better but I was never as quick at it as some of the girls were. I had to do it with very concentrated care because I was afraid I'd destroy the whole pile of cloth.

At home I baked bread for them and everybody liked it – my mother would give a farl to one or other of the neighbours because it had to be eaten fresh, the flour was still very bad. I wanted Mary Brigid to take some into the training college but she said there never was butter on the table, just melted margarine brushed over sliced loaves so that lumps of it solidified again in the holes in the bread.

My mother was depressed about my father. I asked could I go with her to see him and she hedged for a week or two. She told me she was afraid I'd get infected but at last I persuaded her that it wasn't right for me to stay away. I went and I was sorry I did. He didn't look as I had pictured him now and again down the years. He was thin and limp. His eyes closed from time to time. He took no interest in me. My mother said, 'And here's Martha.' He made his eyes look at me but he did not recognise me. He said, 'How are you?' and he held out his hand to me to shake but it was so cold and dead I wanted to drop it straight away. She sat by his bed holding his hand, running her fingers up and down his, rubbing them gently, pushing his cuticles down on his nails to make the moons show. He lay there saying her name over and over again. She was a bit embarrassed with me there and she tried to consult with him about practical things, what did he want brought in, what needed washing, but he didn't pay any heed to that. 'She's happy now,' I thought, 'she has him all to herself. She has cut us all off from him. He doesn't know there is anybody else in the world and he doesn't care.' I knew that wasn't fair even though it was true. So I could sympathise with her one evening when she was tired after her day's work and Danny wouldn't stay in to do his homework and she had to get two buses to go to the hospital and she complained, 'Your father just doesn't want to get better. He's happy lying there with me tearing across the town to see him. Nobody needs to be really sick with TB any more. Everybody else is getting cured with this new medicine. They've done everything for him and he won't get better.' She looked at me then and said, 'I suppose you think I'm blaming him in the wrong.'

I said, 'I think you're just worn out,' because I didn't want to get into trouble for agreeing with her or disagreeing.

When she was gone I began thinking what it meant that nobody any more need die of TB. The Mulhollands would no longer be a sick family. Hugh would not die before he grew old. And I started to cry with pity for myself sitting lonely over the little fist of a fire that was all we could get in our Belfast street because I had cut myself off from the country where I had lost all of my friends because I had been too careful of myself, afraid. I remembered walking back from Miss Rankin's house after returning her bike the day before I came home. I had tried to thank her properly but she was in a hurry out and she had no time for me. All along those wee roads back to the Moss I was hoping to see Hugh to say goodbye and afraid he might not want to stop and speak to me. My heart thumped every time I heard a bicycle behind me but it needn't have bothered because there was no sign of him.

I wiped my eyes and got up and did the dishes and told myself I didn't want ever to live in the country anyway and I went off to the public library and laughed to myself at the number of books and no compliment to anybody.

A letter arrived from the solicitor in Lurgan one day telling me to call and see him about Maggie's will. It wasn't easy for me getting to Lurgan when I was working but a succession of people came to Belfast that year on state visits – Churchill, Lord Montgomery, Princess Margaret – and we'd get time off when we were supposed to go down town and cheer. On one of those days I took the train to Lurgan without telling my mother or anyone. He told me he could sell the house and farm for three hundred pounds. I was dumbfounded. How could anybody pay that amount of money for such a place! But I told him to go ahead, only to keep the money for me until I was over twenty-one so that there would be no complication. I told him I had no money at all to pay him any fee so he could pay himself out of the three hundred pounds, and I didn't want any correspondence unless it was absolutely necessary because it would only give rise to trouble. I thought he was a bit insulted at first but he just said, 'Well, you know your own mind all right,' and showed me down his stairs carpeted with a beautiful blue and gold pattern of the 1932 Eucharistic Congress badge on the landing and a mahogany banister and polished brasses on the big heavy front door. I was tempted to go into a café on the main street and treat myself to a cup of tea and a bun – I had often imagined when I was visiting the hospital how nice it would be if I could do such a thing. But I gave up all my wages every week to my mother and she gave me back what pocket money she thought was sensible, and the train fare had made a hole in it.

'Where have you been all day?' my mother asked when I came in. She'd been sewing and the kitchen was littered with bright-red cloth in a splashy white design and the brown-paper patterns she made herself instead of buying packets of patterns in a shop.

'Just a train ride to Lurgan to get out of Belfast,' I said. 'What would I have done in Belfast with the shops shut and the police out in force and the crowds waving Union Jacks?'

'I thought you might have helped me with this,' and she waved round at the sewing, 'now that you're a kind of a professional.'

She smiled at me and I felt very small. 'Don't you know quite well I can't sew. I never was any good at it and I never will be,' I said, cross.

She started to cry then, the first time I'd seen her cry since after my granny died.

'I've done everything all wrong for you,' she said, and I said nothing. 'I meant to do the best I could for you. I thought the country would do you good when you'd missed out on schooling. You were such a puny wee thing when you went to stay with the aunts. I couldn't see how to make your cheeks rosy and I thought that country cottage was a godsend. You think I just got rid of you – I know you do. And now you're home I thought we'd be friends and you could have a nice easy job sewing, not hard on your health like the mill, and we'd do the sewing between us every night and get my business going right when the coupons come off cloth and we'd have plenty of money. I was looking forward to it. I was depending on you.'

She kept wiping her face and I was so sullen, so sulky. I went to put on the kettle, thinking to myself that when she'd said all this and got it off her chest she'd think things would be different. But my life would be just the same. Of course I was guilty about not mentioning Maggie's will or the money I had coming to me. I told myself I had to obey Maggie's dying wishes and the thought of the money cheered me and I wanted her to be cheerful too.

'I'm all right,' I said, clattering cups. 'Don't be worrying about me. But I'll never be able to sew – you may resign yourself to that,' and I let on to laugh.

'Do you want me to find you another job?' she asked in a washed-out voice.

'Not at all. It's all right, I tell you. A job's a job and they won't sack me. I'm not great but I'm always in time and I never take a day off and I do what I'm told without answering back so that makes me better than most of the girls.'

I thought sometimes of the great freedom I'd had in the country and the lovely open sky and then I'd remind myself of the cold, and the days at the end when I didn't know would I have a bite to eat. I was afraid that some day when I was in a bad temper I might tell my mother about those times. I knew if I did she'd never forgive herself or me.

It was different when Mary Brigid was home on her holidays. She got home on Saturday afternoons too and my heart would lift on Saturday mornings with the thought of it even though she was no sooner in than she'd be gone again and I'd be cleaning up after her before I could enjoy her being there. She was home for two or three weeks at Christmas and then a week at Easter. She didn't like her college much, not the way she'd liked her school, but she just made fun of it all. She imitated the nuns and the lecturers and some of the girls with accents that were strange to her. She talked in other people's voices more often at that time than in her own and I got to know them the way I never had from her letters. She'd tease my mother and have her laughing and she'd boss Danny and make him get up in time in the mornings and do a bit at his books. She couldn't get him to bed in time at night because he wasn't in, and she said she wasn't going to lower herself going looking for him. Sometimes when she wasn't there my mother told me to go and find him and I was miserable walking along the streets by myself when other people were standing in groups and the boys whistled after me. I hardly ever found him anyway. I didn't love him the way I should have loved my only brother. He annoyed me with his surliness and his laziness. I raged when he would not better himself with his education but if he was out later than he should be and I wondered was he hurt or in trouble or in bad company I would get a tight anxious feeling round my heart and I would clasp my hands and pray that he'd be all right. When I think now of worrying then, I could laugh. Such a quiet time it was, but there were boys who stole and boys who broke lamps and that was trouble enough.

I didn't feel sad when my father died – I was too anxious

about my mother for anything else to matter. I had to make myself remember how good and loving he had been to me when I was a wee girl before I could cry at all. I didn't want the neighbours to say I was a cold strange girl with no heart. Mary Brigid seemed much the same as me – she hadn't known him for years either. But poor Danny cried and cried. He stayed in his bedroom and he ate nothing. Uncle Jimmy gave off to him, told him he was a big fellow, he had to be the man of the house from then on. But after Mass when he was to take his corner of the coffin he couldn't stand. His legs folded up under him and two men had to half-carry him out of the church. My mother's face was all pursed up, disapproving. After the last of the neighbours had gone out of the house that evening Mary Brigid made tea and toast and brought it up to him, and I heard them talking after a bit, she nice and quiet and sympathetic and his deep boy's voice full of tears and flying off the handle every now and again.

'He didn't know Daddy was going to die,' Mary Brigid told me that night in bed. 'He was waiting for him to come home. Mammy never told him he was so sick.' I believed it. My mother and he never really talked to each other. She snapped at him, he jibed at her letting on she was stupid. When they were together at meal-times I could feel the resentment between them taking away my appetite. And of course he didn't stay in the house any time he could escape.

'Why did he never go to the hospital at visiting time?' I asked.

'Mammy said it was as well to keep a boy of his age out of sight of the authorities or they'd only intern him when they took the notion,' Mary Brigid said and I wouldn't know if my mother really believed that or was it just another ruse to keep my father to herself. 'Danny says he hates being in a house with all women. He wanted my father to keep him company. Now he's condemned to live with us.' I laughed but Mary Brigid went on, 'It's all right laughing, Martha, but what would you feel like with only men in the house, nobody to talk to, nobody to know what you meant without explaining?'

'Terrible,' I said, not having had a man in the house since 1940. 'What'll we do for Danny?'

'We'd better get married,' she said. 'Our husbands would even things up. Mine can sleep in here with me and yours can put up a bed in the kitchen.'

'God, wouldn't it be awful?' I said. 'Imagine Mammy coming down the stairs in the morning and looking at us with that face she puts on,' and we started to laugh, hugging each other. On the first night my father was in his grave we fell asleep giggling.

eight

Mary Brigid wasn't long about getting a husband but of course they didn't live in our house. They got a house of their own and were like a pair of children furnishing it – they were so happy.

Before that, when she started to teach in a school down near the docks, it was lovely to have her living at home. She'd be finishing her day's work before me and she'd clean up the place and have it shining – I never knew anybody so particular about a clean fireplace. She didn't do much in the line of cooking with us although she managed it grand once she had a house of her own. Sometimes she'd be asleep in the chair that I always thought of as Granny's, with her head down on her arms, and when I'd come in she'd waken and sit up with her cheeks pink and her eyes clearing. I'd have jumped up feeling guilty about sitting down in the daytime. Teaching, to begin with anyway, took it out of her. She was small and thin, and she had big numbers in her class. For the first two years, until she was approved of, inspectors used to come into the school and she got all worked up each time although she made fun of them afterwards with their Yorkshire or Scottish accents.

She was always buying beads and earrings – mostly in Woolworth's because she had very little more money than I had in spite of all the years she had been at school. Once a string of pearls she was wearing broke and scattered all over the classroom. The wee boys she was teaching helped her to gather them up and they were sitting down again, squashed in their desks, when an inspector walked in and said he'd watch while Mary Brigid gave a lesson. She was struggling away, trying to keep control of the whole sixty or so, only every few minutes a boy would dive off his seat to the floor and stand with his hand up and a pearl in it all pleased with himself to say, 'Miss, wee bead!' He didn't laugh at all, that inspector. Mary Brigid was in stitches telling us at home. Myself, I would have been mortified.

Later on when she was teaching an older class of girls she had an inspector from the south – Tipperary or Limerick, she told me. He was a Protestant minister's son and very nice and gentlemanly, not like the Englishman who looked at the crowded infant room and sniffed, 'They breed like rabbits round here.' Mary Brigid was teaching geography about the Six Counties when he interrupted her and said there was no need to teach them about local geography – to let them teach her. Then he said to the children, 'How many girls have fathers or brothers working in the shipyard?' Some of them said their daddies were dockers but he said he wanted to hear about shipbuilding and they looked at one another without saying anything. He turned to Mary Brigid and asked, 'Do they not understand my accent?' and she said that was no trouble to them only none of them had anybody working in the shipyard except now and again when there was a rush of work. Suddenly it dawned on him that he'd heard Catholics didn't get these jobs and he went pink and embarrassed so that Mary Brigid felt for him and began talking about the rocks in the Cave Hill that belong to everybody.

At least you would think the Cave Hill belonged to everybody but one Easter Sunday Mary Brigid and I went for a walk up there. I hadn't wanted to go. I didn't go for walks much after being used to the bike in the country and it made me sad to remember how my father used to bring us, but my mother said, 'Oh, for goodness' sake go on, Martha, don't be always sitting around.' There were policemen all over the place because they were always afraid at Easter there'd be a meeting of Republicans on the Cave Hill – a mixture of Wolfe Tone and Easter 1916. We had a drink at the spring and went round the top of the quarry. Then we saw somebody, a man, lying below the caves. We ran down to tell the policemen so that they'd help him but they grabbed us and said we were acting as decoy. One kept me there on the path and the other made Mary Brigid go with him. By the time they got to the place the man had gone off, and the two policemen took our names and address and told us we might be summoned. Mary Brigid was in a state because if she was brought to court she might lose her job. We never heard another word about it but for a good while I worried about her, not for myself. I had nothing to lose. I was so fed up I used to imagine myself in court saying all kinds of grand things about freedom and a united Ireland and then being a martyr in gaol.

When I said anything to Mary Brigid about Ireland she'd tell me to quit raving, and I never dared mention anything like that to my mother because of my father's ruined life. I was disgusted with Danny when he went to England for a while to work in Dagenham after being at secondary school and passing his exams. He didn't stay long. He was lonely for his friends. He was hardly ever in the house. He got bits of jobs one after the other and when my mother was after him for money towards the house he said he got nothing at home but his breakfast. It was true. He ate out of the chip shops.

I was jealous when Mary Brigid began going out with Brendan. He was a teacher too in a school near hers but his home was in Tyrone so he was in digs and had time to put in at pictures and concerts of one kind or another and plays. I was jealous of the grand time they were having together. I was jealous that she had somebody to love her and I was jealous of him that he had so much of her thoughts and company. I had a bitter nasty taste in my mouth because I was ashamed of myself. I was glad she was happy but I just wished I was happy too. When she got engaged and they were settling to buy a house my mother was in the seventh heaven of delight, sewing things for her and buying cloth at bargain prices to make curtains. For the wedding itself my mother would have dressed the whole street for nothing, she was so pleased about it all. You'd have thought her own married life had been a bed of roses, she was so enthusiastic about it.

I began thinking of Hugh Mulholland. It wasn't that I had never thought of him since I came back to Belfast. Sometimes I would be thinking about him day after day for weeks at a time with his face suddenly appearing in my mind but then again for months I'd forget about him. It was sixteen miles to where he'd lived and as far as any chance of seeing him went he might as well have been at the South Pole. I never heard a word from the country. Then when the factory was shut for the July fortnight and Mary Brigid was away on her honeymoon I met him on Royal Avenue. I thought first I'd slip by and pretend I hadn't seen him because my heart began a terrible thumping but he saw me and smiled, a bit shy. 'How's the country?' I asked. 'How's everybody in the Moss?'

'Ah, they're all grand, just grand. But I live in Belfast now, you know. I married a wee girl from Belfast and she wasn't going to live in the country. Belfast girls don't stay in the country.'

He was laughing a bit but I couldn't look at him. I had to keep my eyes on the traffic and the people on the footpath or he'd see the shock I'd had. 'Did you get work here?' I asked and he told me he was driving a lorry and he had a house on the Falls Road.

'I'm sure I'll see you around,' he said and I told him I hardly ever went down town. Big drops of rain began to fall and he held out his hand to feel it, and then he said, 'It's raining!' with a kind of exuberant indignation and rushed away. That's the last time I ever laid eyes on him although I heard later on that he had his own lorries after a while and, when all the rebuilding started, he got rich.

That night in bed I cried and cried with such a pain at my heart because it might have been all right for us if only I hadn't been so fearful. He hadn't died. He wasn't sick. He was still full of life. And I knew the way he said 'a wee girl from Belfast' that he had been fond of me the way he now was of his wife. I moped for weeks with a stuck-on smile on my face to deceive my mother but I'd catch her looking at me, worried. 'Oh dear, Martha,' she said once, 'have you any life at all?' and I hadn't.

She wouldn't let me go often to visit Mary Brigid and Brendan. I liked to help out with the things they were doing to the house. They had the kitchen furnished and one bedroom. They had no money for carpets so they rubbed the floors with emery paper and then wax to smooth them. They were busy scraping off old

71

wallpaper and paint and I thought I could have been useful to them but my mother said, 'Leave them alone. It's lovely for them to have a house to themselves. It's something I never had.' She didn't go to see them unless she was asked specially, so that one day when I went over with a load of curtains she had sewn Brendan said to me, 'Does your mother not like me, Martha? Does she not like Mary Brigid being married to me?' I told him she thought he was wonderful and Mary Brigid wonderful too to be married to him and expecting a baby and teaching instead of working in a mill. I told him she appeared a bit stiff and stand-offish but when he got used to that he'd appreciate her.

She fretted and prayed all the time Mary Brigid was pregnant but Mary Brigid told me there was nothing to worry about. She felt fine and the doctor said everything was normal. She gave up her teaching a month before the baby was born and said she was glad to sit down. Brendan looked after her so carefully and with such delight that any normal body would have rejoiced for them. Without any great fuss she had a wee girl and when I went to visit her in the hospital and saw her there in the bed and the baby, a wee tiny small Mary Brigid, in the cradle beside her I started to cry and sat there with the tears tripping me. It was lucky there were no other visitors or I'd have been disgraced and embarrassed. I was her godmother and they called her Emer because Brendan was all for Irish names. I was allowed to go and visit them after they brought the baby home because they weren't alone any more and also because my mother wanted to hear every report about the baby even though Mary Brigid wheeled her over in the pram every Saturday and Sunday.

Brendan was amazed that I knew nothing about all these old names – Emer, Eithne, Maeve and Fergus – but I never found any books about Cuchulain and the Red Branch Knights or the Fianna in any public library in Belfast. Brendan tried to tell me the stories while Mary Brigid gave the baby her bottle but Mary Brigid was impatient with him. She knew all the stories beforehand and what she wanted was to talk to the baby and have us all look at her every blink. Then he lent me his book of

72

Yeats plays and I read them over and over again. I didn't think much of Cuchulain. I didn't believe all this 'honour' stuff that made him kill his friend and then his own son. I didn't like the way he treated Emer, his wife, and I was sorry my wee godchild was called after her even though I liked the sound of the name. I didn't say that to them, and of course I didn't say it to anybody else because I would have had to explain too much. I thought then I'd learn Irish not to be so ignorant and I enrolled for classes in the Ard Scoil, remembering Miss Rankin and her shelf of Irish books behind the green curtains on the glass door of her bookcase.

nine

One thing I noticed if I was in a crowd at that time in Belfast –
you'd never see any nice-looking men or boys. The girls looked
all right but if the men had nice faces they were small and squat
or if they were tall their faces were uncouth. So I wasn't expecting
to meet anybody handsome at the class and Dermot Hughes
didn't look much really – mousy hair, greyish eyes, not tall. But
he had a clean collar even though it was a Tuesday. Most people
that I knew in those days did with one clean shirt a week, starting
on Sunday. One pair of socks too, it must be admitted. He was
wearing a lovely soft shirt with green and white checks and a
dark green wool tie. His clothes were shabby enough apart from
that so I knew he couldn't be rich. Most of the people in the
class were from around the Falls Road, some from away up at
the top of it where the houses were far better than Mary Brigid's.
They were nearly all in pairs or groups talking and laughing. I
was alone. When I said to the girls at work would they come to
learn Irish they said, 'Is your head cut, Martha Murtagh? Are
you mad?' Dermot Hughes was on his own too and when I
smiled at him he came over and sat beside me. When I asked
him why he had come to the class he said, 'My mammy told
me,' making fun.

The teacher was an old man in a tweed suit and a little gold
ring in his lapel to tell people he would like to talk to them in
Irish. The cloth round the ring was all pricked and plucked
because he kept pulling the ring in and out on its long pin. He
spoke in Irish the whole time so I understood very little and he
had old charts with pictures on them of a man or a woman or a
child or a table with writing in Irish underneath. He'd point to
the picture and say the words over and over and then he'd ask
somebody, '*Caidé sin?*' and we were expected to say '*Is tabla é*'
or '*Is bean í*'. I couldn't see how I'd ever learn to read a book in
Irish but Dermot kept me laughing with the remarks he passed

74

about the pictures. At home-time it turned out that he lived about ten minutes away from our house, in the next parish. It was a warm September night with a half moon and stars so we walked home and I told him about the Yeats plays and he didn't make fun of me. He asked where I worked and he said he was out of a job. 'But I'll get one soon. I'm bound to. I can drive a van. There's always work for anybody that can drive a van.'

He never worried. Some weeks he had a job, most he hadn't. We went home together from the Irish class but he never asked me out to the pictures or anywhere else. My mother was delighted, making plans for me straight away. Women coming in to be fitted for their dresses were asking me, 'When are you going to get married, Martha? Has she somebody hidden away, Annie?' Until I met Dermot she looked uncomfortable and she'd say, 'Oh, I suppose if she had somebody I'd be the last to know,' and they'd say, 'Some fella with a big farm in the country, eh Annie,' and I'd make myself laugh and say, 'Surely. A gentleman farmer.' Most girls I knew got married before they were twenty but I was well on into my twenties at that time. I had no notion if Dermot wanted to marry me and I didn't know did I want to marry him. We'd just walk home together or get the bus if it was raining and we'd talk and he'd never touch me. Still I looked forward all week to the class. Mary Brigid didn't think much of him for not bringing me to all the things she and Brendan had gone to before they were married but I said he had no money mostly, and she said, 'Even so.'

He lived with his mother. He was the last of the family, born when she was in her forties. The rest were married either in Belfast or in England. Some of them had been gone before Dermot could remember. His mother had only lately stopped working in the mill. Now she was on the pension. When the class finished in June he asked me would I come one Saturday and meet his mother. We went over the brickfield that separated our street from theirs – I suppose they made bricks in it once but I don't remember that. It was a stretch of hard bald clay at

75

the side near our house but at his end there were slopes of rubbish dumps covered with grass and weeds. It wasn't a dirty place really. His street had houses just on the side facing the dumps and Dermot's was the last house in the row.

'The Hugheses have lived in this house for hundreds of years,' he told me, which I knew couldn't be true because it wasn't a hundred years old but he believed it so I let him get away with it. 'Nobody else ever lived here except our family,' he said, all proud of it. 'When it was built my father's father's father (you can go back as far as you like) got it and we've never missed a week's rent.'

It was an ordinary wee house with yellow bricks set in over the door and round the windows, but inside a lot had been done to it. The old black fireplace that we had in the kitchen was gone and a beige tiled surround and a neat grate was in its place. There were two vases of red paper flowers on the mantelpiece and a clock between – it was only a little ledge. I wondered how they cooked or made tea even. Then Dermot opened what I thought was the back door but it was into an extension they'd built. They called it 'the back kitchen'. There was a gas cooker with four rings and a grill, and below, an oven. Beside it there was a sink with hot and cold chromium taps. I knew then I wanted to marry Dermot.

A woman I know once told me she made up her mind to marry her husband whom she wasn't very keen on when she saw his sister's wee baby boy sitting up smiling in his pram. She thought if she could have children like that she'd be happy blessed. And she was. She never minded the husband much. That was all right, I suppose, but I knew I wanted to marry Dermot when I saw his gas cooker. I'd never had an oven. There came into my head all the things I could bake. Mary Brigid had a cooker much like this one, but she didn't like baking and when I brought over flour and things once she raised her eyebrows at the mess baking made on her shelf even though I cleaned up after myself.

'Have you had a seizure or what?' Dermot said because I was

just standing looking with my hands clasped. I turned to smile at him but I heard the door bang and his mother stood inside with a yellow pastry box in her hand – yellow cardboard tied up with red string and a nice loop for her finger. She put it down on the table in the kitchen and pressed the palms of her two hands on her chest because she was out of breath.

'Oh, daughter, I meant to be here before you and get your tea ready,' she panted.

'I'm always early for everything,' I said – it was true too. 'I can't help it, even when I start out late I arrive early.'

She hung her coat on the back of the door and reached up for her hat and pulled out the hatpins. She stuck them in her cardigan alongside about a dozen other pins, safety pins, straight pins – all sizes. She was an old woman, more like my grand-mother than my mother. My mother was straight, slight, quick. But Mrs Hughes had permed grey hair and a wrinkled face, her neck a wreck and her body bent so that nothing seemed firm. She wasn't exactly fat – just loose.

'Seeing you're in the back kitchen, Dermot,' she said, 'put on the kettle, will you. I need a cup of tea.'

'You always need a cup of tea, Ma,' he said and she sat down and poked at the fire.

'Isn't it a nice wee grate?' she said and I admired it honestly, thinking of our black monstrosity with the bars broken and a gully trap filling the hole at the bottom. I wondered why we never did anything, anything at all to our house.

'And the back kitchen,' I said, 'I think it's lovely. It must have been a very big job.'

'Aye, it's grand,' she said. 'Joe and Tommy sent me the money from England and Charlie put it all in for me. He had his two boys to help him.'

I didn't know who they all were. Dermot never talked about his brothers and sisters, nor wouldn't even when I asked him. He was clattering about with the kettle and a tray. He stuck his head round the kitchen door. 'What cups will I put out?' he asked his mother.

'The good ones, don't you know right well,' she told him. 'The china ones Sadie brought home for me last year.'

He put out two little cups and saucers all flowers and curlicues and a big white delft one for himself. She heaved herself up then, leaning on the arms of her chair and on the backs of the others when she passed. She put the wee buns on a squarish plate to match the cups. Some of them had pink icing, some yellow. We never bought buns in our house – my mother would have thought it a terrible waste of money. Dermot put out two big slices of white loaf bread for himself with butter and bright red jam. I had never seen Dermot eating anything before and I was a bit horrified at the way he wolfed it down, concentrating. The old woman chewed with her back gums even though she had no teeth missing in the front. She ate three buns one after the other while I was nibbling one. I enjoyed the new flavour while I was eating it but it left a very cloying aftertaste and while I was trying to get rid of that by drinking plenty of their weak tea I wondered did they always have meal-times with the only sound the noise of eating. My own throat swallowing the tea nearly deafened me. My mother, Mary Brigid and I had plenty to talk about since each of us worked in a different place. And old Aunt Maggie and Bessie talked away even though to finish up with Bessie used to tell us the same thing two or three times during our dinner or tea. 'What would they all think of this old woman?' I wondered. Dermot was nice to her, cleaning up round her, brushing up the crumbs with the wee brush and shovel from the chromium companion set on the hearth, and then going into his back kitchen to wash up.

'Will I help you?' I asked. 'I could dry.'

'Ah, not at all,' he said. 'I'm used to it. Expert.'

I was awkward sitting down again, trying to make conversation. I said about how near the mountains looked from here but she was surprised. 'Daughter, dear, they're miles away!' And of course I knew that – they just looked more immediate than from our house, something to do with the way the land sloped that

78

had the newish estate built on it, streets and streets of it on the other side of a river.

'I'll run out and buy some cigarettes,' Dermot said, 'I'll not be a minute,' and I was left there.

'What do you think of this place?' the old woman asked me. 'We've got it nice, haven't we?'

'I think it's lovely,' I said, 'I love the cooker.'

'Do you love Dermot?' she asked but then she gave a cackle of a laugh so that I didn't have to answer her. 'He's a good boy, you know,' she said and I said oh yes I could see that. Then she said, 'He wants you to marry him.' I said nothing because I couldn't think what to say. 'I'll not live for ever,' she went on. 'I was old when he was born and I'm older still now,' she laughed. 'But I've always looked after him and kept him lovely. He likes things to be nice – clean and tidy. He'd manage all right by himself but he'd be lonely. I'm always here now but when I used to be in the mill he'd have everything all ready for me to come home to. He'd be a very good husband.'

'He doesn't have a job very often,' I said to stop her making him out such a paragon.

'And what man does?' she demanded and I thought to myself – Mary Brigid's husband does. 'You'll keep on working in the mill the way every other woman does.'

She was quite tart so that I contradicted her. 'I'm not in the mill. I'm only in the Rayslip's factory. I don't earn as much.'

Dermot came back then and gave his mother a cigarette and lit it for her and one for himself. I never smoked in my life. I said I'd have to go home and I went out by myself. I didn't let him come. I didn't want him saying anything. I needn't have worried. He never did ask me, just took it for granted that we were getting married and I went along with it because I could see no other future for me.

I often thought wouldn't it be lovely to love, to feel a smile all through you when you'd see a man, to want to be in his arms not just for comfort. Some very ordinary people do. My mother did, I think, although it didn't do her much good or bring her much happiness. Maybe I might have been like that with Hugh Mulholland, but maybe I mightn't. Mary Brigid and Brendan seemed to enjoy each other's company but they didn't look really like lovers. Sometimes Mary Brigid was impatient enough with Brendan. And Dermot and me?

ten

We went to Bangor for our 'honeymoon' of one night. Weddings were in the mornings in those days and after the breakfast there was too much of the day left to go up to Dermot's house with the old woman sitting there. So we took the train to Bangor and walked along the front in a bitter east wind. The shops were all shut because it was Easter Tuesday so we had no place to shelter and there was some kind of a junior Orange parade banging drums and waving Union Jacks. The café we went into for our supper was nearly empty with chairs upturned on half the tables.

'Are you shutting early?' Dermot asked the man who took his order for sausage and chips.

'No,' he said. 'We never took them down today. No need. Nobody here. Too cold.'

We were glad when it was a decent time to go to the room Dermot had booked. It was a bigger bedroom than I'd ever been in with windows facing down the lights along Belfast Lough. It was very stiff and straight and cold so that we started off in bed just hugging each other to warm up. It wasn't like the great wedding nights I have read about in books but we managed all right. When he had gone to sleep and I was lying there with my face at his back I got the cotton smell of his new pyjamas and I felt happy, really happy, until I searched in my mind and found I was remembering the smell of wee girls' dresses pulled over my head in the days when my mother and father kept us so safe. I fell asleep telling myself that was not what I was to expect from being married to Dermot.

I expected great things all the same, great unspecified things, so of course I was disappointed. Dermot was always nice, listening to all I had to say and smiling at me but he didn't have much to say himself and in the house his mother was always there. I went back to my job the same as ever and Dermot had a job driving a banana lorry so we weren't badly off but when I suggested going out to the pictures or some place on our own he wouldn't hear of it. 'What would we want to go out of our nice warm house for? Anyway, my ma would be lonely.' I knew she wouldn't. I knew she'd be happy enough in her own kitchen on her own. Her old friends came to visit her during the day while we were out. But I never was any good at asking for things so when Dermot didn't jump at the idea of taking me out I dropped it. He'd sit there twiddling the knobs on the wireless so that it rattled and scraked. He never listened to anything for long but he turned it on the minute he came into the house. The old woman talked to herself or to me, I never was sure which, but when I was reading a book I couldn't concentrate on it for fear I would miss something she wanted me to hear. I asked Dermot would we go back to the Irish class but he said there was no sense in that. So I visited my mother once a week and Mary Brigid once a week and for fear my visits would look like a sign of discontentment I always brought them bread that I'd baked.

To begin with I baked far too much – soda bread and wheaten bread. I put caraway seeds in the white bread because Bessie in the country did but Dermot looked at it in disgust and said, 'I hate seeds,' and his mother said, 'Daughter, them seeds would stick all round my teeth.' So I left out the seeds but even so they reached for the sliced pan loaf from the breadman and only ate my bread if there was no alternative. My mother had a very small appetite but Danny could eat any amount I'd bring, although he never put on weight. His forehead was big – 'a noble brow' Mary Brigid used to tease him. His whole head was big really as if he had been meant to grow but something had stopped him. He wasn't often in when I visited, just my mother busy on her sewing machine. She was happy that we were both married and only worried about Danny. One night he was there and she was asking him did he never think of going to England again to get a proper job seeing he had plenty of schooling. 'I'm never going back to England,' he said. 'You couldn't wait to pack me off to England when I left school but I'm never going back.'

'And why not?' she asked, bridling. 'Plenty of men get good jobs in England. Your two uncles were glad of the jobs they got there.'

'I can't get over you wanting me to work in England,' he said. 'Didn't England kill my father?'

She got all red and annoyed and said she didn't see how he could blame just England – that it was the Unionists.

'It's all the same,' he said and off he went.

She was upset. 'I don't like to see him hating like that,' she said. 'It's not right and it'll do him harm. It's no wonder he loses jobs if he says things like that.'

Dermot was lucky that he managed to hold on to his job – it was supposed to be only temporary but it lasted for ages. He didn't hand up any of his pay packet. I had been used to giving over my pay packet unopened to my mother and Mary Brigid cashed her cheque and handed over the money. Danny was thought very bad for not giving any but nobody looked to Dermot for his and he just kept it. It was no wonder he was able to buy nice shirts for himself. The old woman and I ran the house between us, she with her pension and me with my pay. It didn't work out very well as I never knew what she would buy. She didn't like to be asked. She was close about what money she had and what she got from her other sons and daughters. She had a big black handbag that she took with her everywhere, even out to the toilet, and was always getting into panics about it – 'My bag! My handbag! Did anybody see my handbag?' It would be on the floor beside her feet or stuffed in between her and the arm of her chair. I wondered did she think I was looking into her things or even stealing them but I held my tongue. It was her house. She wasn't nasty to me or anything. She didn't take a lot of notice of me except that I was to do everything for Dermot's comfort. Dermot thought his comfort was very important too. If he wanted something he felt he had to get it straight away.

When I was pregnant with my first baby he said, 'It won't make any difference to you – sure it won't? We'll just go on the way we are?' His mother wasn't excited either. 'Aye? Ah well, I had nine.' Mary Brigid was expecting her second and Emer was a lovely wee thing smiling away and talking thirteen to the dozen. She wasn't walking and everybody used to carry her about and when we said to her, 'Hello Emer,' she said, 'Hello Emer,' back until she realised she was Emer. She had a dolly that Brendan's mother had given her. It was too big for her really. 'Big heavy girl,' she'd say, hugging her. I imagined my baby would be another Emer only I'd call her Elizabeth maybe or Margaret after the two aunts in the country. I'd have her to love and to talk to and my mother would make her wee dresses like Emer's. Once the baby began to move inside me I kept up a conversation with it. I called it 'wee love' but it was a girl baby I was talking to. It took my mind off my tired legs and the pain in my back later on when the baby was heavy.

'You have an enormous big son,' the doctor told me. He was smiling and so were the nurses. I often marvelled at those smiles at each of my births and them delivering babies day and night. After a while I made myself waken up and ask, 'Did somebody tell me I had a boy?' They told me yes, nine pounds four ounces, and me so small and how had I managed it? I didn't feel any of this wonderful joy I'd read about. I felt as if somebody had kicked me up the Cave Hill and down again and I was cold and hungry and I was landed with a big son. No wee dresses and again nobody to talk to. I don't know would it have been any different if it had been a wee girl but I felt each baby to be a terrible weight on me, a terrible responsibility, from the first minute they were put into my arms a terrible worry. I remembered a headline in Miss Killeen's class – 'Success is the reward of unremitting vigilance' – and I never felt I could let up.

I was surprised at how pleased Dermot was with him. 'What are we calling him?' he asked me.

I hadn't thought of a boy's name. Mary Brigid had taken my father's name for her new son so I said, 'How about Patrick after your father? Would it please your mother?'

He shrugged his shoulders. 'I don't think it would make a bit of difference to her. I don't think she ever misses him. Any time she mentions him she calls him "your da". His old cronies used to call him Paddy all the time.'

'He's not to be called anything but Patrick if that's his name. I won't have it shortened.'

Dermot laughed. 'You'll have your work cut out to make that stick.'

I didn't tell him that Patrick was the name of my lost grand-father. So Patrick he was christened and I brought him home and started boiling bottles and making up feeds and wakening up at two and six in the mornings and having him starving half the time because he was big, and roaring and never sleeping during the day. Mary Brigid when she had Emer had shown me how important all the sterilisation was and I kept him spotless.

Of course I had to go back to work. Dermot kept telling me how likely it was that he'd get paid off any time and his mother seemed ready enough to mind the baby. She was fond of him, but I was terrified of all the pins in her blouse and cardigan and of her old woman's clothes. I mentioned it to my mother and before the week was up she appeared with two lovely big white calico aprons for the old woman. 'For the nanny!' she said, holding them out smiling as if to get a child used to the idea. 'Let me fit them on so that I can turn up the hem,' and while she was fixing the length of the aprons she'd ask the old woman for the pins out of her chest. 'Aren't you great to have all the pins ready for me?' she said, lifting out all she could get at. 'You don't want any of those sticking in young Patrick. Did you ever hear of a baby getting a pin stuck in him? A real case? I never did although I was always warned about it. You had nine. You must know all about it.' The old woman was as pleased as Punch.

One day I came home from work and found her getting ready to give the baby his bottle. She had heated the bottle in the kettle, she had on her clean white apron and Patrick up in her arms struggling – he was very big and energetic. Before she saw me she took out the bottle and to test for its heat didn't she put the teat up to her mouth and suck it and was about to put that into his mouth when I leapt at it and snatched the bottle and the child. I boiled up the teat again in a pot of water, letting it boil and boil while Patrick roared and fought with hunger and the poor old woman sat there looking stricken. In the middle of it Dermot came in and stood around with a miserable face. 'What's up with you?' I asked in a bad-tempered voice.

'I got paid off,' he said and all I could feel was relief because I could make him do things right for Patrick where I couldn't trust the old woman.

My mother was angry with me. 'A bit of charity doesn't go amiss,' she said. 'You'll be old yourself some day.'

'But she has such a terrible mouth,' I said. 'It would be bad enough anybody but she's always sucking peppermints and she has those loose teeth. When they annoy her she ties black thread round them to pull them out but she can't keep up her courage to give a jerk to the thread. Imagine that mouth and then Patrick's.'

My mother loved the babies, mine and Mary Brigid's. She relaxed with them and smiled, just watching them, but she wouldn't admit I was right. 'How do you think all the babies were reared up to now? We didn't know how to boil everything in sight and nothing happened you.'

It didn't matter. I couldn't bear the thought of it so I gave strict instructions to Dermot what to do and that he was never to let his mother near Patrick's bottles. 'If you do,' I told him, 'I'll give up my job and then I'll know things are done right.' Dermot just shrugged when I told him of her heinous sin but I knew he resented my criticism. I'd get a nasty look every now and again and she took to glaring at me and muttering to herself when I was around. I know I treated her badly but I know too I'd do the same at any time in my life, only later on maybe I wouldn't do it so roughly. She didn't turn against the baby, which made her a bit of a saint. She'd put on her white apron in the afternoons and have him lying across her knees with his nappy open and let him kick against her hands and bounce his bottom up and down. She never cared where the fountains scooted to, just laughed, an old woman's throaty chuckle.

Dermot was great with him. He talked to him, bathed him, fed him, pushed him out in his pram, smoked cigarettes all over him. I had the sense to say nothing although sometimes I'd wave away the smoke irritably. Anyway I was expecting another baby and I soon had two boys with just the year between. It was too much for Dermot. He didn't keep Declan as nice as he'd kept Patrick. When I'd come home there'd be a stale smell of milk about him. I'd wash crusty bibs and matted woollen jackets at night but in winter-time there was no place to dry so many and the old woman's kitchen that she had fixed up so nicely before I moved in was festooned with nappies and vests and pull-ups and jerseys and pyjamas. She didn't complain and indeed I was glad of a hand from her many a time getting them to bed for Dermot would fling off out as soon as I came home. I didn't blame him for he had enough of the house all day but it meant we were never together.

Except in bed. I would want to go straight asleep because I couldn't stay awake, or else just talk while lying in his arms, but he was not content with that. After I had the first two boys the doctor explained to me when I might take the risk and when I'd be bound to get pregnant but one thing I noticed – when we were supposed to be safe Dermot just turned over and snored and when it was really risky he wanted to make love. I was anxious to please him. My own enjoyment was far less than the terror I had afterwards that I might be pregnant again. I was nasty to him many a time but he never held it against me, never took insult, always was ready to try again until we had four boys. Then I said no, never again.

I told myself he never loved me really. He wanted a wife and his mother told him to find one and I was the nearest he found. We got on all right. He was amiable enough. In bed he used to tell me he loved me and I'd tell him the same – the words came out of me somehow without me wishing to say them. But once we had the four boys and I said no more, that was a blight.

Sometimes he would smile at me and I would think, 'Oh he does love me and he is nice and I can't refuse him,' but the thought of the four boys born before we were six years married turned me hard-hearted.

He did his best with them but he didn't listen to them much or spread his attention over the four of them so I thought they were neglected and I was afraid they wouldn't turn out much good. He said that I thought he could do nothing right and if I was so particular why didn't I give up my job. I said all right as soon as he got work. So he did, driving a bread-van this time, and he said it was a permanent job so long as he was satisfactory. I was glad to stay at home with my children, glad to leave the factory where I never got skilled. There were two drawbacks. First he thought because he was a man out at work and me a woman staying at home he had a right to marital comforts. I had to keep him straight on that. The other was lack of money now I had none of my own.

eleven

A great many of my neighbours were shiftless people, not a bit like those I was reared with even though it was the next parish. They couldn't keep over from the night before enough bread for their breakfast. Even if they meant to, somebody in the house finished it off, just because it was there. Or maybe I'm too hard on them. Maybe they were hungry. Certainly they were kind generous people ready to divide their last crust, but bad managers. They bought sliced wrapped bread even though it was dearer. What's a penny? they said. So Dermot had to rise very early to put their loaves on their window sills before the man they hired came along rapping the doors to waken them. He'd go round then on Saturday evening to get paid – that's if they were in when he called or had any money. That was the only part of the work he didn't like. Apart from that he loved it. He'd talk about the lovely smell of fresh bread that he met in the morning air when he was going to the bakery and even when he opened the back door of his van on his deliveries. He talked so much about it he made me a bit jealous. He described too the fine new machinery they had even though it was a small bakery. Just about then Mary Brigid's husband Brendan brought me back from Tyrone where he visited his parents, a big old griddle the size of a bicycle wheel.

I was so pleased I was nearly crying while I thanked him for it, and I wondered why I had never taken Bessie's when I just pulled the door behind me and left all. In my mother's house I had baked farls in the frying pan on the gas ring but I stopped that when I got to the oven in Dermot's. Now I was delighted to go back to the griddle even though it was so big it took up two gas rings turned low, which wasn't very economical.

I still had bread to give away only it wasn't easy for me to get over to Mary Brigid's or even my mother's if I had to dress up four wee boys before going out. I used to be tired before I'd get out the door. So I gave big farls of soda or wheaten bread to my neighbours and they were killed giving me bits of things back so as not to be all take and no give. My mother was visiting us one night when Lena McGuinness called to give me half a dozen eggs because I had given her bread earlier in the week.

'I know you like country things,' Lena said to me. 'I just brought you a wee few eggs that I got from down the country.'

I knew looking at the eggs that they were out of the shop and also that they cost far more than the bread would. 'Ach, you shouldn't have bothered,' I said all embarrassed. 'You're far too good. Dermot and the boys will have them for their breakfast. But you should have kept them for your own family.'

'Sure, I have dozens!' she said and laughed and we both felt awkward.

When she was gone my mother said, 'Martha, would you ever think of selling your bread? It would help you with money.'

'I couldn't,' I said at once. 'How could I take money from neighbours?'

She didn't say anything more but I thought about it.

Money was a terrible annoyance to me. I had the children's allowances but that was all I could count on without asking Dermot. I hated asking Dermot. It wouldn't have mattered what kind of man he was, I would still have hated it. But Dermot had been spoilt. He thought his money was his own. His mother had never asked for any and while I was working I didn't either. Now I suggested that he give me housekeeping money out of his pay. He looked miserable, asked what amount I would suggest and then handed it over, shading his wallet with his hand so that it would be hidden from me. But the next pay day he didn't offer any and I had to ask again. That happened week after week and if I was tired and cross with the children and the housework I yelled at him many a time, and oh dear, the resentment I stored up so that it was like a big lump in my chest. Then other times he'd bring home a bag of apples for the boys or a cake for his mother now that she went out so little or a specially good cabbage for me, looking so pleased with himself it was hard not to love his happiness, but it didn't keep money in my purse for the ordinary milk and flour, meat and potatoes.

Dermot's mother had stopped buying things. Her daughter Theresa collected her pension for her every week and brought it to her intact and warned her to put it all away in the handbag. So she did. My mother would tuck a couple of pounds into my apron pocket any time she could and I felt like throwing my arms round her neck. She studied patterns to make boys' clothes, a thing she had never done before, and she made corduroy long trousers for them and dungarees and even wee duffel coats. I had to buy jerseys and shoes and underclothes. Mary Brigid couldn't pass me on hers because her children were smaller than mine.

After she had Emer and Seamus she had a good gap before she had another baby and as soon as Seamus was two she got in a woman to mind them and she went back to teaching. That meant she had her own money and Brendan's both coming in and they sat down every month and worked out how all the money was to be spent, all even and open. She was always telling me this, as if I didn't know it was a great way to do things, but Dermot was very different from Brendan. They didn't like each other much. I'd see the looks they cast after each other. I was jealous of Mary Brigid many a time and she knew that without me ever saying anything. She knew she had a far better life than me. When she'd get something new for the house she'd be apologetic. They bought a long table for the sitting-room to put in front of the couch. 'I know we don't really need it,' she said, showing it to me when I visited, 'but it's handy to put a tray on, or if Brendan is marking exercise books he can put them in two piles.'

'You both work hard,' I said, stroking its lovely polish. 'Why wouldn't you have nice things?'

'Isn't it a pity you didn't go to secondary school?' she said often enough. It wasn't her fault and no way could she be blamed.

In spite of the hassle I liked to go over while the children were up. If I waited till I could go alone at night I could only look at Emer asleep in her cot but if I got my four ready in the afternoon I could arrive just after Mary Brigid came home from school and Mrs Power had her hat and coat on to go. Emer would sit beside me then, very close, very neat with her two hands between her knees if she wasn't showing me her books or her dolls. She was like a little fairy, so light to lift compared to my solid sons, and she spoke precisely as if all belonging to her had not been reared in a backstreet or in the wilds of Tyrone. Seamus was a placid happy child and enjoyed playing with my four. He and Patrick were great friends but sometimes they ganged up on Declan and teased him and jeered at him. Declan had a stammer at times. That worried me and afterwards I brought him to a speech therapist but it never cleared completely. There wouldn't be a sign of it for weeks and then when something upset him or he was nervous, he would get dreadful paroxysms. His own name was a difficulty – D-D-D-Declan – and Patrick's the same. Owen and Eamon were no trouble to him. Mary Brigid got him to sing and whistle to make it better and we'd think it was working and then another day he'd be as bad as ever. I worried about him going to school. I worried about them all going to school but Mary Brigid and Brendan assured me there were no teachers like Miss Killeen any more. I hoped they were right.

Just the same it was a relief when each one went off up to the huge school where hundreds of wee boys were all bunged in together. They were happy enough. They were used to playing with the other children from around the streets. They all came to play on the dumps. They climbed up on all fours and slid down on their bottoms or else dug holes and threw dust at one another. Sometimes horrible things appeared and the children had to be kept away. There was one miserable winter with snow and hail and frost and black ice all during January and February. A poor old pony and donkey that lived there had big plasters of frozen snow stuck to their coats while they stood for hours with their heads hanging. Then March came in with lovely warm sunshine and high blue skies hazy at the edges and when the noon Angelus rang it sounded lazy and sleepy, too luxuriant for Lent. One day I saw a knot of wee boys standing round looking at something on the ground. I wiped my hands and ran out still holding the damp towel, and there lying was a dead cat. The snow had melted off its back fur but there was a bad smell and when I looked close the whole inside of it was seething with maggots darning in and out. It had to be buried deep at once. We had trouble borrowing a spade – for who would own a spade that hasn't an inch of garden? – but we made do with shovels. I lost my peace of mind about the dumps.

Dermot's mother had taken to her bed during that bad winter. She said she couldn't keep warm any other place and I sympathised with her and tried to get heat into her bedroom by keeping a big fire in the kitchen and lighting the gas oven, leaving the door open even though it took a lot of money. Her married daughter Theresa took to calling every morning. For years she had collected the pension money each week but apart from that I had seen little of her as the old woman preferred to go to Theresa's house for the outing. I'd met her first at our wedding, in bright blue with a veiled hat. She had a big broad bottom and a very firm way of planting her feet as if she was taking possession of the ground. 'Be good to him now,' she told me, 'I reared him,' and, because I didn't know what to say, I laughed and it was the wrong thing to do. She gave me a very nasty look then, but I tried to forget that. When the attention began I thought it was very nice and hoped I would be as good to my mother. But she'd tut-tut at her mother's bed and whip off the sheets that were only just on and ask me for clean ones. 'My mother was always very particular,' she'd say. 'You can't expect her to lower herself now.' She'd look round the kitchen bearing the signs of rearing four wee boys and she'd sigh and ask, 'What have you done to my mother's lovely kitchen? How on earth did you manage to destroy it?' It wasn't destroyed but I knew it wasn't the lovely neat place I had been brought into and I felt guilty and sorry for the poor old woman who'd had her 'babby-house' done away with and her peace and quiet robbed from her.

Even when the good weather came back she didn't want to get up. She wanted her door shut to cut her off from the kitchen. I know she didn't warm to me but she never criticised me and when Theresa did she'd say, 'Leave her alone now, Martha does her best.' She didn't smile at me though when she said it. She smiled at the boys all right and they did messages for her but a little of them was enough for her. She tired of them very soon. Theresa didn't leave me alone. She never even tried to be nice to me. She said I wasn't giving her mother enough to eat. 'She loves cream buns,' she told me. 'Why don't you buy her some cream buns for her tea? She'd eat them.' I told her I hadn't the money for cream buns. 'What do you do with all Dermot's money?' she said. I baked a rhubarb tart and the old woman was sitting up in bed eating it with a spoon and enjoying it because I had put so much sugar in it, but Theresa snatched it from her. 'Don't you know rhubarb is pure poison to her? Who ever heard of giving rhubarb to an old woman? Maybe you want to see her dead and buried?' I never answered back. I don't know why. It's not that I'm meek but I just never answered back. I'd tell my own mother, just for the joke, some of the really outrageous things she said and my mother always asked, 'And what did you say?' She never got used to the fact that I said nothing. 'Why doesn't she take her mother into her own house?' she'd say. 'I'll just ask her that!' I warned her not to say anything of the sort.

The old woman used to be very fond of my mother but, trying to avoid meeting Theresa, my mother cut down her visits. At first I'd be asked, 'When is your mother coming to see me, Martha?' and I'd pass on the message and my mother came. But as she got more muddled she forgot all about my mother. She called my children by her own sons' names. They always corrected her indignantly but she couldn't make out what they were talking about. That summer all her sons and daughters came home from England at different times to see her because Theresa told them they had to come and say goodbye. Half time

94

she didn't know who they were and they tired her. 'Isn't it time you were going home to your own house?' she'd say while they were sitting with her. Theresa was in her element, bossing her mother and her brothers and sisters and me, and while they were around, fussing and weeping about her poor old mother and how good she had been to them. Dermot didn't assert himself at all. He'd go out to the pub with his brothers, just nod to his sisters and keep away mostly. Sometimes he'd take the boys off from under all our feet.

On the first cold night in September the old woman died – in her sleep we said, but who is to know? She was settled down for the night looking no different and in the morning I found her dead and cold. I sent Patrick round to Theresa's at once because I knew she should be here but I was trembling at the thought of how she would attack me.

'You mean to say you didn't stay up with her?' she demanded the minute she came through the door. 'Nobody with her to hold her hand? Nobody to run for the priest?'

'You know she was anointed ages ago and the priest visited her regularly. You know that,' I said because Dermot was standing in the scullery door with the razor in his hand, saying nothing.

'Nobody to put the rosary beads in her hand?' she went on as if I hadn't spoken. 'And her so attached to her rosary all her life. Never left it out of her hand if she had an idle minute.'

I thought to myself I had never noticed. One of the things I missed in this house was the night-time rosary. I had been used to it at home and in the country with the two old aunts but when I moved to Hughes' house they didn't have the custom and I was too cowardly to suggest it. I made up my mind to start it with the wee boys as soon as the funeral was over.

Theresa went into the bedroom and began hunting round the bed.

'What are you looking for?' I asked.

'Her handbag,' she said. 'The insurance policy is in it. I need to bring it to the undertaker's.'

95

I told her she'd find it in the bed beside her mother's body. She turned back the clothes and grabbed it. She glanced at her mother's face. 'Her mouth's open and her jaw a bit dropped. If you'd been watching you'd have been able to fix that up for her. I don't know how the undertaker will manage it. But it's his business.' She didn't look in the bag at all, just went off with it.

'There's pounds and pounds in that bag,' I said to Dermot when she went, and he looked at me without understanding.

'How will we do without her?' he said.

'Who? Theresa?' I asked, but he wiped away tears with the towel and I was glad somebody mourned his mother. I tried to hug him but he took no notice so I frowned at the boys to make them stay away from him. It was Sunday, otherwise he'd be gone to work without knowing a thing about it till all was settled.

When I came back from Mass with the children Theresa was in charge. I went straight into the scullery to bake. 'What are you stuck in there for?' she said when she found me.

'I wanted to make sure there's something to eat for everybody that calls,' I explained.

'Sandwiches is what you need,' she said. 'You should be boiling eggs and slicing tomatoes and buttering bread,' she told me, flinging things round the scullery.

'Go ahead if you like,' I said. 'You were reared in this house. You know where things are. I just want to have baked bread for people.' I had an ulterior motive. I had made up my mind during Mass that I would do as my mother suggested – I would sell my bread. It was to do with seeing Theresa making off with her mother's handbag full of pension money and while she was boiling my eggs and using my bread and butter and tomatoes with such slapdash generosity and bumping into me at every turn I thought there was nothing in the world I wanted more than money of my own, that I made myself and could do what I liked with. If the friends of old Mrs Hughes who called during the next few days liked my bread they'd remember and come and buy it when I began to sell. I even left out caraway seeds because there might be some that objected to it. They all said it was lovely, especially hot with the butter melted on it the way Bessie and Maggie had served it to us in the country after the blitz. Theresa's sandwiches were left in stacks. She took them home to feed her own family.

twelve

When the poor old woman was buried with her husband in Milltown and the fuss was over and Theresa gone, I went to see my mother to get her help. I needed money and I didn't know anybody who had any but I thought my mother might have a wee bit put by. I had to buy flour and milk and a couple of small griddles because the big one from Tyrone was grand for our family but the farls made on it would be too big for economy. She was all excited and anxious to help. 'If only it was sewing, I'd be more use to you,' she said and I asked her to make me a white coat and a big white band to keep my hair away. She gave me money but was insisting that I get the flour through Dermot at the bakery. I said no, I wanted to do it without him.

'But you can't, you know,' she said, 'you're a married woman. You can't do things all by yourself. You have to let your husband give a hand.'

'Any profits have to be mine,' I said.

'That's no way to talk. You never saw your father and me grasping over money.'

'That's because you were in charge of it all,' I said. 'You were always in charge of the money. I remember!'

'It was the way Seamus wanted it. He said I earned the bulk of the money so I was to deal with it. Mind you, I had the worry of making it stretch. He gave me his and took a wee bit back for those books of his and the cigarettes before he gave them up.'

'Well, that's not the way in our family. If I do this and make money, it'll be mine to spend the way I think fit. So I'll buy the flour I always buy, only more of it.'

Her lips were all pursed up with disapproval but she couldn't know how spoilt and selfish about money Dermot was and how different in every way from my father. I took her hand in my two and squeezed it. 'Do you ever read any of the books?' I asked her to change the subject. 'Now that you have peace.'

They were on a high shelf in the kitchen where they had been put when we were children and might have damaged them.

'I try now and again,' my mother said, sighing. 'At night in bed I try the odd book but I can't keep my mind on it, even the one on old-fashioned clothes that he bought for me particularly. I look at the pictures and they just seem daft and I start puzzling how the dresses could be made and I forget about the book. It doesn't tell you things like that anyway, not things I want to know. Books don't, I think.'

'They take you out of yourself,' I said, but I'd tried explaining that before and it was no use. That was not the way she lived. She wasn't like me or Miss Rankin in the country. I wondered was Miss Rankin still alive. I would never go to the country, never again.

I felt guilty borrowing money from my mother when I had three hundred pounds with that solicitor in Lurgan. I didn't know at that time that I could take just what I needed. I thought I'd have to take it all at once and I knew it would disappear in food and clothes for the boys. I wasn't going to touch it until I had things planned to do with every penny of it. I wasn't really a miser.

When I told Dermot what I was thinking of he laughed, 'I wonder how long it'll last,' but he got me two boards – one to put under the window to display the bread and the other for across the hall to serve as a counter. He knew how to arrange these things. I just had a vague notion from seeing Jenny O'Neill's sweetie shop and others in this neighbourhood. 'There's not going to be much room for us when you've this fixed up,' he said but I told him I'd clear away before he came home in the evenings.

I got up at four the first morning and I lit the oven and put my two neat griddles on two gas rings. I mixed one go of bread for each and watched them baking. I was impatient thinking they'd never be cooked. I had the dry ingredients ready in my big delft bowl, yellow on the outside, white inside, but I couldn't add the buttermilk until there was a griddle empty or room in the oven. I tried to calm myself, sniffing the lovely warm smell of baking flour. The oven was less bother because it cooked golden-brown all the way round but I knew people would buy more griddle bread. It was necessary to turn the farls on the griddle, first one flat side, then the other, and then balance them on each of the three edges in turn until all were cooked. If I hurried them they could end up with a dark grey seam of uncooked dough in the middle.

I had to pause to cook Dermot his breakfast. He ate a fried egg and fried bread every morning except Friday when his egg was boiled. The frying pan took up the space of one of my griddles but I was determined that he would have nothing to complain about. I had to have enough baked to serve to people who wanted bread for the workers going out before eight o'clock. I stopped then until I had the children ready for school, washed and fed. When my boys were young I made sure they had proper meals. If I didn't see about it myself they forgot or didn't bother. If I was sitting with them at the table, talking and laughing and fixing things up, they'd eat away. They all grew up fine and healthy, thank God, except for Declan's stammer. Likely they'd have grown just the same if I had left them to forage for themselves when they were hungry but I couldn't risk that then.

After they were gone to school I turned back to my baking, some wheaten bread, some soda, a few with caraway seeds. The women came in groups and I got into the way of enjoying their company but that first day I was afraid of bread burning in the scullery while I was serving at the hall door. I was through my first consignment of flour before I had bargained for, and people were still looking for bread when it was all sold. I had to avoid that or they would stop coming. My mother and I had worked out a fair price for the bread, counting the cost of flour, butter-milk, soda, salt and gas, and most seemed happy enough to pay it though there were a few always to complain. I had a bit of money at the end of each week, not a lot. I didn't take any account of my labour and by the end of each day I was ready to drop. When the boys were in bed I went to my bed too and sank into sleep. Sometimes I couldn't remember pulling up my second leg into the bed! Dermot never wakened me. When the alarm went off in the morning I jumped up because if I didn't I'd have fallen asleep again. For years I never had enough sleep but I didn't mind, really. It mattered more to me that I was managing. Now and again I'd say to myself, 'Am I mad? What do I do it for? Why don't I give it all up, all the hassle, and live on Dermot's wages like any ordinary wife rearing her children?' But I knew I didn't mean it.

I didn't work on Sunday. One of the priests from the monastery called just as I was taking off a batch of potato bread – I didn't bake it every day because of the bother of boiling a big pot of peeled potatoes. I gave him a cup of tea by the fire and hot potato bread and butter. Those priests had very little money or comfort and were always glad of a cup of tea when they visited. The next day the lay brother from the kitchen was down for the same and then the bursar came and asked me would I provide all the farls the monastery needed. I told him I couldn't, I was sorry but I didn't see how I could possibly bake any more and I never had bread at the end of the day. He wouldn't go away and eventually I agreed to bake for them on Saturday evening after I shut the shop and they could collect the bread before bedtime. It interfered with the boys' bathtime because all had to go on in the same scullery. To give Dermot his due, he carried bathtubs in and out from in front of the kitchen fire and wrapped wet wee boys in towels and scrubbed their hair as if it was all fun for him and the children. There was no scolding or tears the way there sometimes was when I was in charge. But we tripped over each other and I made up my mind that, the first chance I got, I'd collect my money from Lurgan and build on a wee shed in the yard so that I could do the baking there.

Another thing I worried about was the way we had the door opening all the time during the day so that the cold got into the house no matter what fire we kept on. I could see no way out of that. We were in the end house of the street and there was waste ground for quite a distance but I could not find out how to get possession of a bit. It stretched up to an old factory that more often than not lay empty. At that time it was working as a canning factory, doing sliced apples in the autumn and rhubarb in the spring and early summer.

The women coming home in the evening called in to buy my bread and kept me late working but I looked forward to them – fat jolly women in a bunch with their fingers wrapped in bits of cloth from the cuts they gave themselves chopping up the fruit. It was part-time work so a lot of them were older women with their families nearly reared. They just wanted a wee bit of money for themselves or to get some job done in the house or pay for a wedding in the family. They were kind to me and asked for 'them seedy sodas' and called me 'Martha, love' and remembered the boys' names and teased Dermot if he happened to be there. They filled the need I had for neighbours. The street had only houses on our side because of the dump opposite and I had only one neighbour, a widower with two children who were very nervous and whom he hectored about. I couldn't stand him. The wee girl had a shaking hand and one side of her face twitched and he'd shout at her, 'Steady up there, Bernadette!' He'd been in the British army before his wife died. He was mean. Everything was for cash in my shop but if a child was sent for bread without money in the early morning I'd be told, 'My mammy'll pay you later,' and she did. But Stanley next door used to send in poor Bernadette with no money and he knew I couldn't refuse such a pathetic wee body. I saw very little of the money for his bread.

thirteen

I wrote one night to the solicitor to tell him I was coming to see him for my money early in the New Year. I told Dermot I was hoping to get some money but that I wasn't a bit sure. The solicitor could be dead – he wasn't young in 1946. He mightn't remember me or might just pretend he had no money for me. I had no documents or anything to prove my claim except my birth certificate and my marriage lines. I would have liked to consult Mary Brigid and Brendan but I always felt guilty that I had hidden that money away from my family. I prepared my customers well in advance for the shop being shut that one day but even so they were coming knocking with their coins on the door early in the morning. I had had a lovely lie-in until seven o'clock and all I could do was turn them away. I gave the boys a lunch to take with them to school and Dermot said he'd be home in time to mind them from three o'clock and to keep the fire warm.

The train left the old railway station in Great Victoria Street and chugged past the back of blackened brick houses much the same as ours except that there were things written up like 'Prepare to meet thy God' and 'The wages of sin is death'. It was a cold day with frost and near Lisburn there was fog so that the view disappeared and trees were only darker shapes in the gloom. After that when the sun came out my heart lifted and I thought maybe it was a good sign. But even in the broad sunshine the frost on the fields didn't melt and the twigs on the bushes in the hedges stayed white like Christmas decorations. There wasn't a soul stirring. The big houses were planted on the tops of round hills with a view right down the valleys harking back to our ancestors on the Cave Hill. I saw very few wee houses like the ones round Maggie's and Bessie's. This was country for big farmers with houses far apart. I was glad that I was back living in Belfast with rows of houses and the smoke tugging parallel black out of all the chimneys and everybody keeping everybody else warm.

I found the solicitor's house without any trouble and walked up to his office on the same blue and gold stair carpet as in 1946. It didn't even seem to be worn out but the solicitor was older, balder, smaller than I remembered.

He smiled at me. 'Mrs Hughes, I should call you now, isn't that right?'

All I could say was, 'Yes.' I could manage nothing more for nervousness.

'I would have answered your letter straight away but you put no address on it,' he said. He was a friendly man.

'I never got letters,' I explained. 'There would have been too many questions. It would have been awkward.'

He looked concerned, because I had given him a wrong impression. I hadn't meant to, but I left it. 'I often used to wonder what had happened to you,' he went on. 'I used to tell my wife about you. You're not quite so thin as you were then.'

'I've had four boys,' I said, smiling.

'You need the money for them?' he asked and I explained about the bakery. He leaned back in his chair while he listened to me and then reached over and shook hands with me without saying anything. He wrote me a cheque and when I looked it was for four hundred instead of three hundred pounds. I said it was a mistake, too much, but he said it was the interest on the money all those years. I asked him about his fee and he said not at all and if I needed to borrow any money for my business to let him know and he'd write to the bank for me.

'Will the bank give me this money?' I asked him, about the cheque. 'I don't know any banks. I've never been in one.'

He explained to me then how I should open a bank account in a bank fairly near me, and leave the money there. I have prayed for him every day since then – Mr McAvoy he was called. He told me that builders generally work on three payments for a job – one-third at the beginning, one-third when the roof was on and the last when all was finished. I should only pay when everything was to my satisfaction. I laughed to myself but I didn't let him see. I thought the man I'd be getting to do my bit of building would have no such notions. I was wrong – he thought he'd get the whole of the money to start off with.

It was Theresa put me on to this man. He had done work for her mother when the brothers and sisters in England had sent money for building her scullery and putting in her fireplace. He was a handyman just, and the only equipment he had was a bag of tools but he could turn his hand to anything and his jobs worked out well in the heels of the hunt.

I showed him what I wanted – an extension with a sink and working surface and space for my flour and meal and a place for a hot-plate arrangement that would bake more farls at a time. I had no money for the hot-plate but I hoped to save up for it. There wasn't a lot of room left in the yard and we had to stay clear of the outside toilet. Dermot didn't want it at all. He said as always that the house had been in his family for hundreds of years and why did I want to change it. I pointed out that his mother had improved it in her way and I wanted to keep the house itself more comfortable for him and the boys and that I only wished I didn't have to have the whole parish coming in our front door bringing the cold air with them into the room that his mother had made so nice. He still sulked and he wouldn't deal with Charlie at all.

Builders think that women know nothing about what they want or what is possible. We didn't start off very well, of course, with him demanding money for the whole job. 'It's the usual way,' he told me. 'It's not,' I said, 'I consulted my solicitor and he advised me on the legal way to do things.' He had to put up with that and he began in great style so that I thought he'd be finished in a fortnight. But when he had the walls up and the beams for the roof, he disappeared. I couldn't go looking for him but I asked all the women coming in if they'd seen him. They told me he was doing a job at a garage three or four streets away. I sent Patrick and Declan round with a note but he put it in his pocket and it didn't have any effect. Ten days later he came round to tell me he couldn't put on the roof until I gave him more money to buy materials. I gave it to him the next day although I had misgivings and sure enough he spent my money on buying stuff for his other job. There was a man in charge there – that was the difference. They think they can play on women. He did return when it suited him and sat up on the roof in the winter sunshine in great good humour. Stanley next door objected to him being there at all and criticised the way he worked, so Charlie got a lot of enjoyment out of dropping things over into Stanley's yard making him jump, and then apologising. When he was doing the plumbing he started spraying hosefuls of water over the wall but I had to tell him it wasn't right and I wouldn't have the man tortured. Charlie was all innocence – it was just that he wasn't as experienced at the plumbing as he might be.

fourteen

Was it a punishment on me when the flood came higher that year than it had ever come before? Flash floods, the papers called them. There was a dirty wee bit of a river between the old streets and the new estate sloping up the hill. They said it came from the mountains but it had no appearance of a mountain stream, just sooty muddy water with all kinds of rubbish in it. We hadn't been troubled by it as they were in the streets near the river. We were a wee bit higher up. A few times the water had trickled in a dirty brown streel up the entry and under the yard door and we had brushed it out and bunged rolled-up newspapers into the space, but this was different.

It had snowed in February and the snow lay in the hills because it was still cold and then a warm rain came and kept on for a week with only an hour or two respite at a time. The river turned into a rushing torrent banging all its debris against the black grille it had to get through before roaring down under the houses in Flaxmill Street. Men went and stood looking at it until the rain was dripping out of their sodden caps and their turned-up collars and the white mufflers they wore instead of shirts and ties if they were out of work. The women worried about it when they came in for their bread. Some of them had boards to put across their doors or plastic bags filled with mud from the waste ground that they hoped to put outside to stop the water getting in. Some of them hadn't. They'd lost them since the last time a few years ago, or the children had taken them away to play with or to throw in the river. Some of them never had anything. I warned the boys not to go near the river. It was hard enough in that weather keeping them in dry clothes and hanging wet jackets and trousers in front of the fire with shoes steaming on the hearth.

Then they were sent home early from school because the river was out on the streets and some children had to wade to go home. Before I stopped working in the factory I had to walk through the flood a couple of times. The water was only above my ankles but the force of its pull was frightening. Most of my customers couldn't come near me so I cleared all away and closed up. I wanted to sit down with the children and help them with their homework or even read them a story, a thing I don't have much chance to do, but I couldn't relax. I kept jumping up and looking out the window. There was nothing to see at the front but gutters of tumbling muddy water tearing down the street and the sodden heights of the dump. But Dermot called me from the back door, 'Martha, the flood's coming into the yard,' and he started to sweep it out with the yard brush. It was too much for him and for my wads of newspaper. Into the new extension it came, no matter what we could do, and seeped up the new bags of flour that were sitting just inside the door. I had meant to buy big galvanised bins to keep the flour and meal in but I had no money left after the building. We should have lifted the sacks into the kitchen as soon as we saw the water but we were stupid. It struck me after a while that I could maybe salvage the flour from the top of the bags but there was such a smell from the water that I couldn't bring myself to keep it. The boys put on their rubber boots to go out to the toilet before bed, and I bustled about getting them off clean and warm so that I wouldn't have to think of what was going to happen to my baking.

Before midnight the rain stopped and a breeze sprang up and the water backed away. I got a bucket of water and disinfectant and scrubbed everything it had touched and when I went out to empty it down the grate I looked up at the sky and I could see between the clouds big cold black shafts with stars.

'It never came into the house,' Dermot kept on saying. 'In all the years it's been in our family the flood never came into the house. I could have told you that. There was no call to worry, no call at all.'

I gritted my teeth and kept on cleaning and then I put a notice on the door, 'Sorry, no early bread. Flour flooded.' I slept in the morning until after Dermot was gone to work. Nobody rapped at the door. I don't know if anybody came. They had troubles of their own.

I went out after the shops were open to buy flour on tick and the remains of the flood were every place – big swathes of dirt on the pavement and in the road and dead rats in the gutter. Some people were throwing out mats and lino that had been polluted and other women were dashing buckets of water through their kitchens. The sour rotten smell hung everywhere. I remembered reading a book about the famine in Ireland and it talked about the smell hanging over the fields of blighted potatoes. At least we weren't starving.

The shop was able to give me only a couple of ordinary paper bags of flour – the kind I had started off with. Mick McAuley who owned the shop said a lot of his stocks had been ruined and it had happened to him umpteen times before because he was far nearer the river than we were.

'Did you ever go to the City Hall and tell them to do something about it?' I asked and he leaned across, tapping on the counter. 'Every time it happens I go and every time I get fobbed off. I write letters to the Corporation and I get no answer.'

'We must have an MP?' I said because I couldn't remember voting. There was hardly ever a contest in our constituency or if there was it was between a Unionist and a bitter Unionist.

'That oul' Unionist! What does he care about us? A major in the British army. What would he know about a dirty flood disrupting our lives? We're just like the natives in India – we should get used to it.'

An older woman called Mrs Holland had come into the shop and she said, 'D'you remember the time a Labour man went up for here? Northern Ireland Labour, not Republican or anything, and they did everything to keep us from getting our votes. Do you remember, Mick?'

'I got my vote in early in the day. I knew you had to or those Unionists would use it up for you,' he said.

'Well, we weren't so well up,' she said, laughing, 'and it was well after eight when we went up to that big Protestant school and the tally man at the gate asked what street we came from and said we'd to go to another school away on the Crumlin Road. Only we saw Eddie MacDaid coming out and he said it was right for us to vote there – we'd have been done out of our vote, because it was over at nine o'clock. Not that it mattered. He never got in.'

'Isn't he in the Corporation, that Labour man, Bob something or other?' I asked. 'I've heard of him helping people get houses even though they were Catholics. He's a good man, I've been told. Couldn't he be asked to do something?'

'Ah, he's old now. He's got disheartened. They'd tell you it's in the nature of that kind of river to flood.'

'If it flooded over the Protestants they'd change its nature mighty fast,' the shopkeeper said, and I took my flour and went off home to bake the wee bit of bread it would do for.

I kept wishing I could do what real business people do and phone the flour mill and order flour. But there was no phone anywhere near us and anyway the people in the mill didn't know me. When I wanted flour I'd get somebody with a van to drive over in a free moment and pay cash. That night when Dermot came home he called to Patrick to give him a hand and in they came grinning, each holding the handle of a plastic bin. I smiled at them, not knowing what was going on. In the middle of the kitchen floor they put it down and Dermot lifted the lid and held it up above his head. In the bin was a big bag of flour, the kind they used in his bakery. My first thought was that he had just taken it. Some people did that. It was well known that the Protestant streets had their houses decorated with bits of mahogany and brass from the ships they were building and I knew of women who took stuff out of the mills even though the management were very strict. 'Don't worry,' he said, 'it's all paid for. I even got a receipt for fear somebody would accuse me.'

I reached for the receipt. 'I'll pay you when I get some money,' I said and he was offended.

'Can you never take anything from anybody?' he said. 'It's a present. I didn't give you a Valentine, I'm giving you this instead.'

'Thank you,' I said, 'oh, thank you. I am grateful.' I felt that he was good, that I didn't treat him properly, that I should hug him and put my head on his chest but I couldn't do that in front of the children and besides I didn't want to change the way things were. If I got closer to Dermot there would be another boy baby to look after by Christmas.

That weekend down by the river there was a bonfire of all the furnishings that had been spoilt by the flood. The young lads went round and got rubber tyres and anything that would burn so that black smoke and then flames spread out over the sky, and then they laughed and shouted and cheered. Some of the windows in the houses nearest cracked with the heat. These things always got out of hand.

fifteen

When Patrick was eleven he got the scholarship to go to the secondary school. I had been praying for that night and day. The primary school seemed a happy enough place but it didn't have much success with examinations. The children had no great ambition because the parents were easy-going, contented once they were able to have enough for their children to eat and to put on. I didn't want my sons to be like that but I didn't want them to be pushed like in the school I went to. There was a choir in the parish run by a musical teacher – a Palestrina choir. There were little boys in it and big boys and young men and this teacher taught them all to sing and in Latin. They sang in concerts and on the radio and they were famous. I wanted my boys to join but they wouldn't, wouldn't hear of it. They just laughed and shoved one another around every time I brought up the subject. I loved the sound of the choir. I could have listened to it for ever. But the teacher died before he was old at all and the choir fell apart.

Mary Brigid's Emer was already at the school on the Falls that her mother had loved. Emer didn't enthuse about it the same way but she liked it. She was a lovely wee girl. She was always reading and she thought her books were so valuable that she brought them over to me to mind while her family were away on holidays because there wasn't room in their car to take them all with her. It wasn't a very big car or a very grand car but they had a great time with it. They went to a cottage in Donegal to spend their long summer holidays. They had four children: Emer, then two boys, and last, a baby girl born the year Emer went to secondary school. My mother offered to make Emer's new school uniform but Mary Brigid said no, she was buying it from the uniform shop because she wanted her children to have all the things she had to do without when she was a girl.

'She did very well for herself, the same lady!' my mother said, a bit offended, and I thought so too but nobody ever was really annoyed with Mary Brigid because she didn't mean to annoy anybody nor did she see that they were annoyed. So it would have been a waste of energy.

It took my mother a long time to get over the fact that I hadn't told her about my money from the old aunts. She was glad I had it and liked what I did with it but after the first amazement there was a glint in her eye any time it was mentioned, followed by, 'And you never told me!' Mary Brigid just said, 'Goodness, isn't that very odd?' She always talked things over with Brendan and in that way she got them off her chest. My mother didn't have anybody but indeed I don't think she was lonely in the house on her own. She didn't have to worry about anybody. Mary Brigid and I were well off and Danny was still in his job at the bookie's and had notions of getting married, although he never did. Poor Danny.

I got my new bakehouse cleaned out eventually after the flood although on damp days I was sure I could still get the smell of it. There was no direct heat because I still baked on the gas stove in the scullery. But when I'd get a good run of baking on the way in the mornings and nobody around but myself and the warmth from the stove and the smell of bread all through my domain, I'd find myself so happy my mind would say, 'How lovely is Thy dwelling place, Lord God of Hosts.' Now that the Mass was in English with the people having a part instead of just the priest and altar boys, there were all kinds of lovely prayers I could hear but that was my favourite. It gave over my place of work to God so that my bits of creation would join in with his. I didn't have a lot of time for prayers but I had a crucifix over the door. The Sacred Heart picture that everybody had with the red lamp was in the kitchen where Dermot's mother had put it. She had got a wee electric lamp. In my mother's house it was still the wax night-light under a red glass dome the same as my grandmother had. It was up high and so it never got broken in those days.

113

It looked for a while in the sixties as if things were going to improve. They even covered over the eyesore of the dump and put tarmacadam on the top to make it into a children's playground. It was amazing to see how long afterwards the seagulls continued to swoop, looking for food in big screeching wheels coming between us and the morning sun. I liked to watch the children on swings and slides and roundabouts in their bright clothes and comfortable long trousers that the mothers were able to buy with their children's allowances. There is no nicer sound to me than children shouting and laughing.

Because of all the children I thought for a sideline I'd make candy apples one September, the same as old Jenny O'Neill used to sell in her shop near us when we were small. I bought a box of yellow apples called Kemps that were sweet and soft and I made up the toffee out of a cookery book Mary Brigid had given me, but to this day I never managed to keep the toffee on the apple. It all slid off so that the bare apple on its stick was sitting in a platter of toffee. I wasted more time and patience on them than enough. Children would chew the toffee and eat the apples but I couldn't charge much and I was ashamed of my failure. I had forgotten what it was like not to be able to do things. Other experiments lost money too but then I could blame my customers' lack of adventure.

The smell from Dermot's bread-van tantalised me because it was different from my shop. His bread was made with yeast. So I got little bits of yeast and tried out rolls and loaves on Sundays. The rolls were fine but the loaves wouldn't stand up properly until I got a couple of loaf tins and then I baked a lovely rich brown loaf with wholemeal and a dessertspoon of black treacle in it. I thought it was beautiful and so did Dermot and the boys. After I'd made it a few times my mother suggested trying it in the shop. So I bought four of the tins because that was all the oven would hold, and put the bread to rise one Sunday night. Nobody wanted it. I told them it was a great flavour but they said, 'Of course it is, Martha, but my man wouldn't touch that.

Just the four soda farls and two browns. That'll be all. No tatie bread? No, I know you don't have it on a Monday. I just wondered.' So that finished that. I baked currant sodas too sometimes and they didn't go too badly, just a bit slow.

The factory closed down around that time and I missed the six-o'clock-in-the-evening rush. I was always in hopes that it would open again for something or other but it never did. It was only the start of the closing down. When the mill my mother worked in closed down I nearly died, thinking my mother would break her heart but not at all.

'Do you not think I've earned a rest?' she said to me.

'But I never saw you take a rest,' I told her.

'Well, I'll take one now. I'm not a bit sorry to end my days in the mill but I'm sorry for the people that need it. The days of linen are done.'

I hate the sight of a closed mill – a big ugly brick building shutting out the light with no reason for being there.

I had been thinking of putting up my prices a bit so as to make a wee bit more profit for myself but with the closed mills I was afraid of losing custom. There were big chains of 'home' bakeries appearing on the main roads. The bread was baked in central places and delivered in vans hot to the shops. The display was very tempting and I didn't blame people for buying there if they were passing, but I got a bit annoyed if they then depended on me for bread at half-seven in the mornings and bought from the other places for their tea. I knew I had no right to be annoyed – I was in business to supply what people wanted. They owed me nothing.

I still had very little time to myself. If I had a minute to glance at the *Irish News* in the evening that was all I got to read. But I had the wireless in my bakehouse and I heard news in the morning when I was on my own, and in the summer of 1968 Dermot got a television. Most of my neighbours had one for over ten years but I thought the boys wouldn't do their homework or read anything if the television was on. Theresa was always talking about the great programmes that were on and the great laughs they all had night after night. She thought I was a spoilsport and that my boys were to be pitied, and she made no secret of her opinions. She was a noisy woman.

sixteen

I had heard on the radio about Catholics beginning to look for civil rights – houses that they were entitled to and local government votes for all. I didn't pay a lot of heed to it. I heard about the Protestant girl in Co. Tyrone being given a house for herself instead of a Catholic family but it was no great wonder. It was the way of life we were used to. In June 1968 when Austin Currie protested and was carried out by the police, I thought, 'He's young. He'll learn.'

But when it was announced that there was to be a big march in Derry on a Saturday in October I said, 'They're foolish. They'll start things up again.'

My mother said, 'It's all right talking, but if you have neither house nor job you have nothing to lose.'

'Do you not remember the state you got yourself into in 1935?' I asked her. 'When you heard there was shooting?'

'State?' she said. 'What state? I never got into any state. I always had to keep myself calm for the rest of you to depend on. Anyway, that was shooting. This is a march with English people coming over. Nobody is going to shoot at them.'

They didn't either but they hit them with batons and we saw it on our television and so did the whole world and there has been no peace since. I needn't pretend that we didn't get a great laugh out of the way the Unionists were disgraced and tied themselves in knots all that year trying to get out of giving a fair deal to the Catholics. The women coming into the shop were in stitches imitating them all – people we had never heard of before like Chichester Clarke. We loved the back-answers Gerry Fitt was able to give them on television, making them look so slow and stupid. Bernadette Devlin was great at that too but I would have liked them better if they had said they wanted a united Ireland. Brendan said that would not have been good policy but I'd always rather have things out in the open. When

I said that to some people in the shop they were surprised. 'Sure, we know nothing about them down there. A whole lot of them talk Irish, don't they? We wouldn't know what they're saying. They don't talk ordinary like us.' The older ones were more likely to agree with me. 'Aye, you're right there, love. Dublin's a lovely place.' That wasn't what I meant either. I had never been to Dublin although during the war a great many of the people in the country had gone there to buy the things we couldn't get and to enjoy the bright shops.

One day, when I bought jerseys for the boys 'made in the Republic of Ireland' and just afterwards saw a big ice-cream lorry up from Dublin, I said to Mary Brigid optimistically, 'Maybe the border will just fade away with people wearing clothes and eating food from one part to the other.'

All Mary Brigid said was, 'You and your united Ireland! Are you always thinking about it?'

'No,' I said. 'I'm always thinking of baking bread and selling it and feeding my family and what they'll be when they grow up but the thought of the border's like a nail sticking up in my shoe. I've got used to it but it's never comfortable.'

She just laughed.

It was great excitement that year. Some people got fed up with it but it was like drink to me – the meetings and the interviews on the television day after day at tea-time when I had the shop closed. Dermot wasn't really interested but he pretended to be to humour me. I had the constant feeling that Stormont was on the edge of the cliff on Cave Hill and something would topple it over.

That was all very well until some of the people in our parish who lived in Protestant streets were ordered out of their houses. I tried not to believe it. I said it was only a carried story. I said maybe they wanted to get into new houses in Ballymurphy and used this as a reason. I talked like a Unionist because I couldn't bear to think of it happening. Then we saw the fighting in Derry and had to believe it but we weren't in any way prepared for it in Belfast and we had no defence when Protestant mobs set fire to all the streets that led off the main road. They couldn't get in as far as us but when I saw all those wee houses going up in blazes and children crying and women screaming and the men in desperation because they weren't able to do anything, I was in a rage. The next day they built barricades across the streets and the young lads were ready with stones and lumps of piping. None of them had guns.

'Where's the IRA now when we need them?' the women said when they came in for their bread, terrified.

'That's not what the IRA's for,' I argued. 'They're supposed to be getting a united Ireland, not fighting Protestants. Anyway, there's no IRA this long time that ever I heard of in this parish.'

'They're for protecting us, so they are. That's what they're for, and fighting policemen.'

'Where were the police last night?'

'Driving round in armoured cars shooting up the Falls.'

By night-time a lot of frightened wee British soldiers were walking up and down all the streets, even ones where we were in no danger. They moved into the empty factory at the end of our street. They had no comfort, no beds to start off with, nothing. And we didn't know from Adam what they were saying. I didn't like them coming into the shop because of their guns, and two or three of them at the one time seemed a crowd. They were cheeky, speaking to me the way no young lad in Belfast would have done, but they didn't mean any harm and they thought they were being pleasant. Some of the women shrieked when they said these things but I just pretended I didn't hear. I don't think they were right fed because they bought up loads of my bread and started wolfing it while they were waiting for their friends to be served. I had to keep bread under the counter for my regular customers and there was a bit of nastiness about that when I'd tell the soldiers I was sold out. I objected to British soldiers in our streets but I must admit that most people were glad of them and were glad too when they got the barricades down.

These were a dreadful dirty mess of sheet metal and cardboard and blocks, and the ashes of fires that the boys kept lit every night. We had to pick our way through and people with prams and old women not too good on their feet found it awkward. Then these lads took it upon themselves to ask people where they were going and why. They didn't all, but enough did to annoy people with their cheek. The corner boys had all moved up to the barricades but when they were persuaded to take them away and moved back to the street corners the soldiers told them to move. Where could they go? They'd been there as long as I could remember. There were growls and dirty looks. I heard rumours that the IRA were recruiting and training. 'A wee bit of shooting out the back,' a woman said to me with a significant look.

'Must be the soldiers,' I said. 'I hope they're careful. I don't like those guns of theirs.'

'Ach, not at all, Martha. Are you daft!' but another woman shushed her.

I had to push down a great excitement. I was daft as the woman said but I could see a united Ireland coming within the year.

The thing that annoyed me most in those days was when people from Dublin would be interviewed and they'd all agree that they couldn't afford to have us. You'd see a lot of poor young Belfast lads with a tricolour and a notice about wanting a Republic trying to block Kennedy Way and the soldiers pushing at them, gently enough then, it must be said. And then you'd see a sleek well-fed Dublin politician or economist explaining how there was no way the Republic could accept a united country because of what we'd cost. At the same time the people from the south were sending up clothes and toys and household things for the families who were burnt out. Bernadette next door showed me herself in a lovely wee brown coat with a fur collar and a fur hat with fur pompoms attached to strings. 'Where did you get the lovely coat, Bernadette?' a woman asked and she said, 'Up in the Hall,' all smiles, and they started shouting in at Stanley, 'Were you burnt out, Stanley? Didn't you get it fixed up really quick?' and they'd laugh to one another and wink. 'Did you hear poor Stanley here was burnt out?' But nobody begrudged it to wee Bernadette – at least she'd be warm one winter.

Then Mr Callaghan came over from London and went round the Falls and the Shankill and Derry and looked sympathetic and agreed about all the things wrong with the government and the police and finished up saying, 'But the Stormont must stay,' and got into his plane and went back to England. We had thought it would be abolished. It was like saying the wicked stepmother had treated the orphans very badly but she was still to be left in charge.

When the explosions began I took them as my protest. They happened at night. Nobody was hurt. They showed we were disgusted at the way things were turning out. They were shops and factories that were nothing to do with us. Broken glass all over the down-town pavements having to be cleared up every morning didn't worry me. It cost the English exchequer. They'd soon get fed up I'd thought. I didn't say this to anybody. When people said, 'Terrible, isn't it – all these places getting blew up,' I just said, 'Oh indeed,' and changed the subject.

The Falls Road curfew happened at the beginning of July 1970 after the Conservatives won the election in England. The people in those wee old streets just like ours were shut in and not allowed out for any messages while the soldiers searched all the houses for guns. They didn't find much – a few old guns from years past and they broke up the houses. We saw it on the television. I was crying, first with vexation and then with pride when a whole army of women with bread and milk came marching down from other streets further up and pushed the soldiers away, shouting at them to go home to England and learn manners. They handed the food in to the besieged houses. I was standing at the scullery door watching the television and not wanting the boys to see my tears when Dermot noticed the state I was in and put his arm round me. 'Don't upset yourself,' he said, trying to get me into the scullery away from the news but I shook him off. 'I have to see,' I told him. Some of the Unionist ministers drove round on a gun carriage gloating over people they had never come among before. The Foreign Minister from Dublin came up to talk to those who had suffered the curfew. He was asked how did he get there and who gave him permission. 'I just got into the car and drove up,' he said. A very quiet-spoken man. Everybody was in a protest with everyone else. We in our part of the town were never noticed much and our street was on the outskirts of the parish so we were never really in anything. But the atmosphere with the soldiers changed. People stopped being friendly with them.

Two young fellows that I had never seen before called into my shop one day that summer and told me I was not to sell any more bread to soldiers. 'I'd be glad to see the end of them,' I said, 'but if I have an open shop I can't refuse to sell to people. There's no way I could manage it.' They left it at that for then. As the winter came on and things grew worse and worse, the growling between the soldiers and the people increased. The soldiers chivvied the people and the boys harried the soldiers. Two different fellows came in asking me what times the soldiers came and how many came at a time. I didn't like being questioned about my business and I thought it was all a bit sinister so I wrote a note to the officer in charge at the canning factory saying it would be better if his soldiers didn't come near my shop any more.

He came to see me and I was very nervous. There were women in the shop when he came in but he told me, 'Serve these good ladies. I can wait.' They hovered because they were killed with curiosity but when he thought they were out of earshot he leaned right over my counter. 'What is all this about my men? You say you don't want them here any more?'

'That's right,' I said, nodding to make it definite.

'Have the Republicans told you to do this?' he asked all confidential.

'No,' I said.

'Have they been misbehaving?' he asked, annoyed.

'No,' I said, 'not any more than usual.'

'What do you mean by that?' he demanded.

'Well,' I said, 'they're never very respectful but I suppose it's just their manners.'

'Are you a Republican?' he asked and I shrugged. I was going to be a heroine but instead I said, 'I am a home baker.'

Other women came in and he strode out.

'What did he want?' they asked. 'What was all that about?'

'I don't want the soldiers in this shop any more,' I said. 'He tried to find out why.' I wasn't sure was it sensible to tell them but I knew some tale would go out and it might as well have a basis in truth.

'What did you do that for, Martha?' one said. 'Getting yourself into trouble. Their money's as good as anyone else's.'

The other said, 'This is really Martha's house, after all, not like a real shop and you wouldn't want these people in your house.'

Some of the soldiers kept on appearing because they were hungry and the smell drew them in but I stuck to my word and refused to serve them. I had a horrible fear of blood in my shop. They shouted bad language at me – words I had never heard although I had seen them written up on walls.

seventeen

When the three Scottish soldiers were shot up in the hills I didn't believe the IRA had done it. First of all I said it was the UVF or the military themselves in a private quarrel. Then I said it was done in self-defence and the bodies had been re-arranged. I never would let anybody say that the IRA had killed them after drinking with them in supposed friendliness. Dermot didn't talk about it and Brendan said, 'It was rough, you must admit. Rough,' shaking his head.

There were plenty of rough things. The IRA talked about 'accidents of war' but it sounded too glib and I felt ashamed, sometimes horrified. A wee girl up the Falls Road was out for a walk with her doll's pram and her baby sister when the baby sister was shot and killed by IRA men shooting at soldiers. I couldn't see how that wee girl could survive such a shock, such a grief. I wondered many a time, down the years, how she was.

Riots kept happening. Nobody ever knew where or when there was going to be a riot with petrol bombs and stones and cars on fire and the dreadful noise of yelling and banging. And people were intimidated out of their houses. We were all right, all safe together, but people living away from their own had to leave or be burnt out. I began worrying about Mary Brigid but she laughed at me and told me not to be absurd, that the people living round her were all civilised and good neighbours.

I was very particular about the boys not being out on the streets. Patrick was sixteen and big for his age but he was doing well at school and wanted nothing but his books. Once he was safe in from the college I could relax about him. The others were different – they just did their homework and no more. They weren't interested in books. Declan was handy and I wished I knew how he could get to be an electrician or a carpenter. He told me he'd just like to work in a garage with cars. Dermot was pleased about that. The other two were just wee tough boys with cropped hair, indignant at the soldiers, but I made sure they were in no trouble.

All summer there was word of internment. My mother said it was bound to come. Brendan said they would not be so stupid. My mother said, 'I can never get over his country innocence!'

I was up baking when it started. I heard the banging of bin lids and the shouting and screaming and later on the shooting. My hands were trembling but I kept on baking. My bread was very bad that day but it didn't matter because hardly anybody came out to buy it. Dermot didn't go to his work. I wouldn't let the boys out of the house.

Danny was shot on the waste ground, shot dead. He had a gun in his hand taking on the soldiers. A priest from the monastery risked his life to go and give him absolution. My mother was so quiet and resigned about it that I remarked that it wasn't really very sad as he had never settled in life and had no wife or children to be bereaved. She attacked me. 'That's all you think a man is. That's the way you live. A man is only to provide home and children and keep you all comfortable. That's all poor Dermot is to you. Danny had no wife and no children and because your father was away all Danny's life from when he was a child, he didn't do anything great and he wasn't very happy. But he was Danny Murtagh, like nobody else in this world.'

Although it gave me a shock that she should criticise the way Dermot and I lived, it certainly wasn't the time to argue with her. I listened to her answering the offers of sympathy. 'He was the best son in the world,' she told one, and to another, 'Never a day's worry or trouble did he give me all the days of his life.' 'He had to be the man of the house once Seamus was taken away. He was only a wee boy but he looked after me and his sisters.' 'He made himself responsible for me – that's why he never married.' There was not a word of it true, not a single word, but there she was telling it all in complete sincerity. I have consoled myself often since, that if a mother can forgive everything and overlook all the bad things, maybe God will do the same.

She insisted he was to have a quiet funeral, no flags or gunshots. She said everybody was too confused with people being interned, and our being blamed for setting fire to a Protestant street over a bit from ours, that they burned themselves, and she didn't want bringing more trouble. Even so when the funeral cars went round a Protestant part of the town to get to Milltown cemetery because that was the normal way, they tried to stop the hearse and threw stones at us. They yelled and howled with ugly faces and it was very debasing and went on for a long time before they just stood back. It was plain to be seen there was no flag. I know some IRA funerals at that time had rows of men stamping their feet behind the coffin and I used to think it barbaric but we were decent and it didn't help us.

I had kept the shop closed, of course, but I had put no notice up because everybody knew I was Danny Murtagh's sister. The day after, an officer came in and two soldiers stood at the door. It wasn't the same officer as had come before because the soldiers were always changing. When we were used to an English accent we got a crowd of Scottish or Welsh. The Welsh were the easiest to get on with, I thought. He wanted to know why I had shut.

'For the funeral,' I said.

'You closed in sympathy with an IRA man?' he asked.

I just shrugged. It was none of his business.

'Was it a gesture of defiance?' he demanded.

'It's a very wee shop,' I said, 'and your men aren't allowed in here so it couldn't matter to them.'

'Were you intimidated?' he asked and I was raging.

'Listen, you,' I said, 'it's my shop and my business and I'll open or shut as I please and nobody intimidates me.' I wouldn't have answered like that if I hadn't lost my temper because with a husband and four boys it's as well to be quiet. He was back the next week asking why I hadn't admitted being Daniel Murtagh's sister.

'You didn't ask me,' I answered.

'Are you an IRA family?' he asked and I told him, 'I didn't know Danny was in the IRA. I never concerned myself with what he did. He was a grown man and could look after himself. Brothers don't consult their sisters on these things.'

'Your father died in gaol,' he said.

'He did not. He died in hospital of TB that he got from being interned during the war for no reason whatever. My father never did any harm in his life. You should just find out how things were here. You're too young to remember it and I don't suppose the English papers ever told you how this place was run.'

He didn't say a word, just turned on his heel and went out and my heart was thumping. Dermot came home in a state that they had stopped him and searched in through the bread, only he had very little left since it was evening-time. I was in terror for Patrick and Declan and I warned the other two they were never again to shout things at the soldiers. The next morning before I started to bake I heard them outside and I opened the door as one was lifting his boot to break it in.

They wanted to know names and ages of everybody in the house and while one was writing it all down the others were prowling around. There wasn't much to search, we didn't have much furniture. But when they got out to my bakery there were the bins of flour and meal, the full buttermilk can and an empty one, and packets of soda and salt and seeds and currants. The griddles were hot and I warned them not to burn themselves but I needn't have been polite because they spilled out everything.

'What are you looking for?' I asked.

'I'll know when I find it,' one said and he kicked the flour bin and cracked it. I never got anything but the plastic bins. I never was able to afford the galvanised kind. They made Dermot and the boys come into the kitchen and pushed them about a bit but they weren't too rough. They went off shouting that nobody would get any bread today, and laughing.

It took me all the morning to tidy up and I had to keep on telling people what had happened. I was afraid to send any of the boys out with the messages for fear they'd be stopped and I was afraid to go out of the house myself for fear the soldiers would come in. After his day's work was done Dermot brought me flour and salt and soda. The rest had to wait till I had got over my losses a bit.

I worked myself into a right state over the boys' safety. Boys and men had been lifted all over the parish and more in the next where I had been reared, and every day there was word in the papers from the real IRA men to say, 'They didn't get me!' There were rumours too of men having been tortured. They were made to stand for hours and hours against a wall with bags over their heads, not allowed to eat or drink or go to the lavatory and when they fell they were kicked up again. I heard on the television a very respected English politician justifying it all – 'But these men are murderers,' he said. And of course they weren't murderers. They were civil rights people and the army were doing experiments on them, that's what it was. At the same time on the television there was a series running about the reign of the first Queen Elizabeth showing prisoners in dungeons chained up with their arms above their heads and telling in gloating detail how they were to be hanged, drawn and quartered. I said to Dermot, 'They must like torture, these people, to have it for entertainment. They call us terrorists!' There were some English people spoke out against it – Graham Greene, I had read some of his books, and a woman on the radio who was usually talking about money. Decent people all over must have felt like them that the English were disgraced, for that particular kind of thing stopped.

I didn't sleep at night. I'd drop off and then waken up shaking. I'd get up in the morning with a terrible dragging feeling that there was another day to be got through. One night when we were both lying awake because the soldiers' lorries were even noisier than usual tearing around, Dermot said, 'Martha, you'd need to see the doctor. He'll give you tablets or something. You're beginning to be very wrecked looking.'

'The doctor can't take the soldiers away or bring us peace, can he?' I said, cross.

'What's worrying you?' he asked and I said, 'It's the whole thing. The whole horror. And I'm afraid for the boys.'

'The boys are all right,' he assured me. 'Patrick is the only one of an age to be lifted and he doesn't look dangerous. He never has his head out of a book.' He laughed a wee bit and took my hand. 'You're not over the shock of Danny getting killed.' I began to say I was not very attached to Danny, never had been, but he said, 'I know you didn't love him the way you love Mary Brigid but a brother is part of you, no matter what you think, and it'll be a while before you're over it. The soldiers breaking up the place didn't help you but they won't do it again now they've searched it once and they know you're not involved in anything.'

'You're a great comfort, Dermot,' I told him and he put his arm round me.

'I'll mind you,' he said, and in a wee while I was asleep.

eighteen

After that I was shaking only part of the time. I could talk myself out of it and my business was coming back a bit. The women in the shop were greatly taken with the rent and rates strikes against internment. It was easy to tell the rent man when he called but the really brave people put up notices in their windows, 'No rent. All spent'. The defiance of my neighbours made me ashamed. When I found out later that Dermot had never stopped paying the rent, I was mortified. The Stormont people decided that they'd take the rents out of dole or children's allowances or whatever they could get at and some people were really hungry. I had to give out bread free, time and time again, but nothing seemed to be deducted from us. I wondered how that was happening and I asked Dermot had he any notion. He said he had always paid the rent into the office and the gas and electricity at the City Hall. I was aghast. 'You went behind everybody else's backs,' I said.

'Supposing they cut off your gas?' he said. 'What would you have done?'

'But it was always me paid the gas bill since I opened the shop. It comes out of the shop money. And I haven't paid any since internment.'

'Well, I'm paying it now,' he said, 'and the rent. I'm not going to have the house taken away from me that's been in our family for hundreds of years.'

I knew I shouldn't blame him but I was ashamed and I couldn't take comfort from him then.

The explosions didn't worry me at first. I persuaded myself they were never intended to hurt anybody. When they did, I blamed the police for not taking up the warnings quick enough. But they did hurt people. They killed people. They blew off legs and arms. They cut faces in great slashes with broken glass. I tried to hide all of that from myself. The IRA would never hurt ordinary people – only the system they were going to pull down. And the border would disappear and we'd be all one united country with our government giving fair play to everyone and the Catholics wouldn't be despised any more and we could have a bit of confidence in ourselves.

Then I saw on the television girls running away from the Europa Hotel because there was a bomb warning. They were hotel workers. They were wearing mini-skirts because that was the fashion. And they were terrified, hysterical. In broad daylight in the sight of the whole country they lost their dignity the way I lost mine secretly in my bed in the dark worrying about my sons. And I knew it wasn't right to do such things to people. It wasn't right to risk killing them or hurting them, and it wasn't right to frighten them. I said so to everyone from then on who mentioned the explosions. When women said, 'Isn't it terrible?', looking at me to see how I'd take it, I left them in no doubt.

But the soldiers kept on doing terrible things, ending up on Bloody Sunday in Derry, and we had no one to look to, no one who cared about us, no one to protect us. After Bloody Sunday we were sure they were going to do for every Catholic district, pick out boys between seventeen and twenty-five and shoot them to show who was in charge. They did it in Derry, thirteen of them, and in the Widgery tribunal we never found out who told them to. It must have been somebody fairly high up, I always thought, not an army man. Armies aren't allowed to take decisions like that, except in Africa maybe. I often wonder is he sorry, that minister, or does he sleep sound at nights, happy that he was never found out, wasn't tried for war crimes or just for conspiracy to murder and put in Long Kesh. The world was shocked and that's what saved us, I'm certain sure, and Stormont was blamed and abolished. We were too far down to rejoice and the IRA said they wouldn't stop their campaign so there was going to be no peace. I was sorry for the Protestants being disgraced when it wasn't entirely their fault. They were just handy people to blame. All the same, things improved for a while.

The soldiers were more polite and they stopped the searches and driving round making noise all night.

Then the sectarian murders started and for a long time nobody was arrested and Mr Whitelaw said things about 'settling old scores'. If men were out at night, not safe in their own area, they were taken away and tortured and murdered. Harmless students or working men, out of works or drunks, all shot and flung in entries or up at Glencairn. Some of them were stabbed and cut and crosses carved on them. Other people were shot in cars in broad daylight going to work and school. Every time in those Troubles that we thought things were as bad as they could be they got worse, more vicious, more terrifying, more shameful. The police always blamed the IRA first. Sometimes they admitted later it was the Loyalists, but quietly so that people in England and the south wouldn't hear. The IRA did horrible things too and we had to admit they were no lily-white knights, but then I'd say to myself trying to excuse them that in France during the war the Resistance fighters did horrible things too and they were heroes in the end.

People in other countries were kind to us, taking children for holidays. In our house only Patrick wanted to go. Declan was happy enough working in a garage although garages were exposed places and dangerous. The two youngest were content with their friends. Patrick went to Germany and Holland and America. If any groups of children had Protestants and Catholics in them money was forthcoming from all over to take them away together. Patrick got on fine with them all but he never saw any of them at home. Even in Queen's when he was doing his degree he never came across any of them again. I could say he never told us much about those holidays but then I didn't have time to listen to prolonged accounts from my children. I know it was a mistake but I got up so early and between baking and serving I was busy all day. At night if I was sitting down I would let on to listen to them but the words would float in and out of my head.

Dermot came home one day with a long face because his

bakery was closing down. It had been losing money for a few years so the two old brothers who owned it just closed up. Nobody wanted to buy it. Nothing depressed Dermot for long, though. He was allowed to keep his van. I asked him what under God he would do with it and he told me he'd build a shed with the back of it for selling the bread in, and the driving part he'd make into an ordinary van. I couldn't think how because I haven't that kind of a mind. Declan helped him with the car part of it and the two of them were covered with car grease night and day, leaving the sink with blobs of grey soapsuds every time I wanted to use it.

'Now for the bread shop,' Dermot said when they had used what they wanted for the van.

'We can't get permission to use the ground when we don't know who to apply to,' I said because I didn't really want to be put out of the house. It was warm and I could rush in and out from the baking if necessary.

'Who minds about permission nowadays?' he said. 'We'll just go ahead,' and he did and nobody cared. Certainly he made a very neat job of it with everything handy but I felt banished out there. Dermot said if he was out of work he couldn't have his house invaded by all the neighbouring women looking at him if he sat down by the fire. He was right and I knew he was right but I couldn't help resenting it. He said he'd serve in the shop if I wanted him to, since he was well used to selling bread, but I didn't let him. It was my enterprise and my money, what little I made in the long run, and I didn't want any complications.

Mary Brigid bought me a record player to keep me company. Her Emer was in a choir in the university and Brendan drove us over to listen to the choir singing the 'Messiah'. I knew nothing about music. I had never heard more than bits of songs except the hymns in the church and the Palestrina choir but I thought the 'Messiah' was marvellous. It was partly the lovely young faces and their enthusiasm but when they were singing the 'Halleluiah' chorus it had all got into my body and was shaking me and driving out tears that I had to get wiped away before anybody would see them. We were standing out on the steps in the cold afterwards waiting for Emer. You couldn't leave young people then to come across the town on their own, and anyway the buses stopped running very early.

'There's music too,' I said, not really meaning to say anything but thinking of all the things in the world that I was missing. The next Saturday Mary Brigid bought me a little Russian record player and Beethoven's 'Pastoral' Symphony – because I loved the country, she said. I couldn't understand where she got that strange notion but I loved the music and I played it over and over and over again. Sometimes my customers would put their hands up over their ears in fun, pretending to be deafened, but I generally turned down the knob when somebody was at the door. She kept on buying me records until I had a stack of Mozart, Beethoven, Tchaikovsky, Handel and Schubert's songs. I asked Mary Brigid why those and she just said she knew I'd like them. They lifted my spirits. I thought of all this lovely music surviving for years and years before these wee streets were built and how it would still be around after we are long dead. That's the way I would calm myself when I'd hear of one atrocity or another. Until one day a crowd of young soldiers flung open the door in the middle of the '1812' Overture and shot a rubber bullet at my record player, knocking it off its shelf, breaking it in smithereens and fusing the electricity. They ran off laughing. I nearly cried with rage. People came round and told me how lucky I was not to have them shoot at me like the poor woman in Andersonstown who was blinded by them.

All my lovely escape world disappeared but nobody else had any escape so why should I? Some women were on tranquillisers and they'd come in for their bread hardly able to make the words come out of their mouths, or count their money or decide what they needed. I don't know how they managed their houses. I think they just sat there. It was no wonder that their sons that they were so worried about ran wild and got themselves into trouble. Mind you, it was hard staying out of trouble. The soldiers stopped men and boys every time they went in and out of their streets and asked their names and what they were doing and where they were going. They had lists of names they'd consult and they arrested people. The crowd that broke my gramophone were a bad lot. They heard Declan's stammer and he was never let pass without being asked his name and all about himself and he'd stutter, 'D-D-Declan Hughes,' and they'd laugh and repeat it and shout after him. He'd come in white with mortification, knowing that when he went out the same thing would happen all over again. I always warned him not to get upset, not to answer back, but I began looking in papers to see if he could get a job in the south.

I saw an advertisement for a lad wanted in a garage in Dublin and I showed it to him.

'What would you think of applying for that?'

'How could I?' he said. 'Sure, I live here. How could I work in Dublin?'

'You could go to live there if you got the job. You'd be away from these soldiers. There's nothing to stop them lifting you.'

'I'm not going to be driven out by them,' he said, and Dermot, all alarmed, took that line too.

'He's all right where he is. Aren't you, Declan? Sure, you don't care about those so and so's? He's got a grand job and he's a great help to me about the place. What would I do if Declan left?'

But he did apply for the job and I put in a wee note to say he had never been in any trouble but was being harassed by the soldiers and I feared for him. He got the job and the good kind people took him into their house until he got a place in a flat sharing with a couple of other young lads. Patrick got a job too as a translator in Strasburg. He did his degree in Queen's University and nobody ever bothered him. He answered the soldiers, taking no real notice of them, and he got his exams and his job and went off to translate German and French.

Dermot hadn't talked to him much as he was growing up but he wrung his hands when he left. 'What will we do, Martha? What'll we do without our sons to keep us company?' I was sad too but relieved they were gone from danger so I told him he'd have plenty of trouble looking out for Owen and Eamon who were left school and had no jobs and no street safe for them between the soldiers arresting and the IRA recruiting.

I used to watch them walking up the street together. They were great friends always, not like Patrick and Declan who didn't think much of each other. When they were at school, carrying up against their chests those big schoolbags that tilted their bodies backward, both at the same angle and their heads up and their chins out, I wondered why everybody didn't see how nice boys were if they were treated right. But they are loyal to one another and quick to see injustice or victimisation. That's what the soldiers and police never seemed to understand. They'd pick on one and be surprised when they brought the whole pack on their backs with a mad neglect for their own safety. That's what frightened me. So at last I got them to apply to the Irish army and they liked it well, especially when they were sent a couple of times to the Lebanon. Mary Brigid's sons were gone too, one to Dublin, one to Canada. That was happening all over because although internment was over, arresting was not and you never knew who'd be lifted. Besides, there were no jobs.

nineteen

Another thing was happening. Streets were knocked down and new houses were built – very pretty wee houses with trees in front. Even in our street where there was no word of that, people were leaving, and empty houses had their windows filled with concrete blocks.

'We'll never leave, sure we won't, Martha?' Dermot said to me, like a child, and I just shrugged.

'Where would we go?'

The children's playground had been abandoned years ago. With the soldiers in the old factory and a police barracks above on the main road, the whole place was railed off with wire and patrolled by soldiers. It was dark and dismal. I didn't blame people for leaving but they were my customers and, although I was still able to make a bit of money, I sometimes had bread over at night and I didn't like that.

'Don't bake so much,' Dermot told me. 'Take things a bit easier, can't you?' But I found it very hard to change my routine. Now and again I'd go outside and lean against the wall of my shop to let the sun shine on my face and feel its warmth on the wall at my back.

One morning Dermot came out of the house and stood there beside me. I glanced up at him and found him looking down at me with the same fondness that he used to have for his mother. I couldn't have that at all. I went back into the shop and started brushing everywhere till the whole place was full of floury dust. I wanted to lock the door and go away up the hills but of course I had to stay and see did anybody come to buy my bread. I wanted to give up but then I'd have to ask Dermot for part of his dole and I couldn't bring myself to that.

I closed up for a couple of days to go to Declan's wedding in Dublin. That was my first time in Dublin and I was lost with the size of it but I loved the relaxed easy feeling of happy people enjoying themselves. Declan's mother-in-law, Kitty McKenna, said I was only romanticising but when I went down town there and saw all those young people laughing and talking and buying flowers I had a great longing for that kind of life to come to us instead of our grim clenched-teeth outlook. I did think there were some daft things, all the same. Declan's wife was a lovely friendly girl called Catherine but the wedding cake was on a revolving stand and the photograph album was really a musical box that played 'Here Comes the Bride' when the cover was opened. Declan was happy and his stammer never appeared even at the altar when I was tensed up for him. The priest was kind and said he wanted to welcome 'our northern visitors' and offered a Hail Mary for 'peace with justice throughout our country'. I could have cried at it only I was determined not to, because I didn't want anybody to think I was one of those mothers we hear about who won't let go of their sons.

On the way home Dermot sighed all sentimentality and said, 'There's the first of them gone. Once one goes they'll all go, like the swallows in autumn.'

'They're gone already,' I said. 'Had you not noticed? We're going home to an empty house.'

'You're very hard,' Dermot said, and maybe I am. I just feel a terrible deep sadness that there is no life in Belfast for our children. Soft words do nothing for that kind of deprivation.

Patrick wasn't at the wedding but he came home to visit us a wee while later and I was so proud of him in his nice clothes and careful way of speaking, until it came Sunday and he refused to go to Mass.

'I don't believe in all of that any more,' he told me when I asked what Mass he was going to.

'You what?' I said, hoping for a second I hadn't heard him right, and then having to hold myself back from shaking him, clawing at him the way I never did on any of them when they were wee boys.

'You go and say your prayers,' he said to me, all tolerant and condescending. 'Maybe I'll benefit.'

When I knelt down all I could say was, 'Oh God,' over and over again, and then, 'What will we do now?'

Then I began to be terrified for him and I tried to persuade God that he didn't mean it, that he was always a good boy, had gone to the sacraments when he was at the university even though a lot of other young lads didn't, and that he'd be all right, he'd come back to his faith. But at dinner-time, while he was telling his father all about Strasburg, I couldn't eat, I couldn't listen. I was appalled. I was thinking he'd be better to have died young and gone to Heaven. He'd have been better with no job, hanging round on the dole but still with his faith. He'd be better knee-capped by the Provos with a disablement only to his body. Anything rather than cut himself off from God. I didn't think it a good idea to say any of these things. He might cut himself off from us too and any good we might be able to do him. Still, I didn't want him to think I had taken it lightly. That night I said to him, 'Would you say the words of the Our Father every day, son, and maybe you'd get to believe again.'

'You're not pretending to be worried about me?' he said. 'That'd be a bit of a change. You never had any time for us all our lives, not one of us. All you cared about was your baking and your shop.' He wasn't bitter about it, just matter of fact, and my heart was thumping with such a weight that I could say nothing, so he went on, 'Anyway, I don't want to change the way I am. You've no idea the relief it is to see through all those things. They're a terrible burden. Not at your age, I suppose, but certainly at mine.' I had a wee bit of hope then that maybe it was over girls but I couldn't ask and I don't know. My peace of mind disappeared that day and won't come back till I see him secure in his faith again.

twenty

There was a phrase they had in England about our Troubles – 'an acceptable level of violence'. It seemed to me, cut off from it all in my bread shop, that the violence came in chunks all more or less horrible. At one stage it was car bombs killing and maiming innocent people in town. Then it was proxy bombs forced on poor innocent drivers who were terrorised into parking them wherever they were told. There were pub bombs, restaurant bombs, there were people shot going to work or at their work, Catholics by Protestants and the other way round. Catholics shot Catholics in these feuds between the different branches of the IRA and nobody was safe because they made mistakes and dashed into the wrong houses. The RUC lifted Catholics and brought them to Castlereagh and tortured them one way or another and they came out wrecks. Hundreds of Catholics were in Long Kesh and their mothers and wives trailing up there in buses with clean clothes and cooked chickens and ham sandwiches that they couldn't afford for their families at home. Policemen were shot and killed, and soldiers, and unfortunate Protestant farmers in lonely places on tractors or in byres, leaving sad old parents with no stake in the future but bitterness. All the time we had the soldiers chivvying us, annoying us. Then there were the hunger strikes and those ten young men leading us to despair. I was ashamed of the dirty protest. We knew that Protestants always said Teagues were dirty pigs. And I didn't approve of the hunger strikes but I thought the British government tricked them, went back on their word, and then when one after another died I felt with all the other women, anguish. It's a word I've read in books but that's the only time in my life I knew really what it meant. I saw the funerals deprived of dignity and the Unionists on the television gloating over each death and the government in England with that stony-faced addiction to 'the rule of law' which meant they could oppress for centuries the poor people of Ireland and India and Africa for their own good. I never in my life hated any person. I never could find anybody I should forgive because nobody ever injured me deliberately. But I had to struggle with my conscience to stop myself hating England, not the individual harmless people, but the whole big thing that was England. There was no use saying it was the government because governments changed and policies towards us didn't, or else they went from bad to worse.

I could do nothing about all of that. It was all out of my reach but when the Provos took it on themselves to bring law and order to the district I got angry. Everybody knew there were boys breaking into houses or tormenting old people. There were always boys who did that and girls who shoplifted or picked pockets. In the days before the Troubles the police were not able to stop it. Sometimes boys were sent away to remand homes and came back a bit worse than they went in. I didn't think anybody had any right to take it on themselves to shoot them in the leg or beat them with hurley sticks or break their arms with concrete blocks. It seemed to me to be savagery but when I said this in the shop a great many of my customers wouldn't agree with me. 'I don't know,' they'd say, 'these boys need to be taught a lesson. They're a torment to the place.'

'They always have been and we've got by,' I said.

'It's easy seen they never robbed you or wrecked your shop,' they'd say to me, and I told them, 'The floods wrecked my shop and it was years before anything was done and the soldiers wrecked my shop and nobody said "Boo" to them.' They just shrugged and said that had happened to them all, and so it had.

I was well known for that view. So the Provos chose to knee-cap that boy at the wall of my shop where the sun had shone on me in the mornings. When they called the next Friday for my weekly contribution to their fund for the relatives, I said, 'No, you're getting no more.' We all gave money. Mostly I didn't mind because I knew some of it did go to the wives or mothers of prisoners. I didn't think the pittance they got from me would buy bombs or guns and although I didn't approve of anything they did they were the only people I could hear of that the English paid any heed to.

'I've come for the money, Martha,' the man said.

'No money,' I said. 'You shot that wee lad's legs at my wall. I object to that. So no money. No more money.'

'Martha, you have to give it. You don't know what you're up to.' He sounded alarmed and he went to the house door and knocked for Dermot.

Dermot came rushing in pulling on his jacket. 'Martha, what's wrong? Have you not got the money?' He turned to the man. 'Business is going down, you know, with the houses emptying. She can't give you money she hasn't got.'

'You'd wonder,' the man laughed. 'People come round to giving in the end.'

I was annoyed at both of them. 'I could give you the money even though my sales are dropping. But I won't. I won't support cruelty.'

He gave me a long look, not knowing what to say or what to make of it. 'See and tell the people in charge!' I called after him and he glanced back, a bit frightened, I thought. Dermot was in a state.

'Martha, are you mad? You're only looking for trouble.'

'I can't let them away with this carry-on,' I said.

'What is it to you? They say he was a bad rip.'

'They'd say anything. I will not watch such a thing without a protest,' I said but I didn't explain it to him. I had never told him nor indeed anybody else about Miss Killeen in school and Lizzie McAteer.

'Do you know what they'll do?' he asked and I could see he was terrified.

'No, I don't. Do you? But it's me they'll do it to, not you. So don't worry.'

'Ach, Martha!' he said and then after standing there, half in and half out of the door, 'give me the money, Martha, and I'll run after yon fella. I'd pay it myself only I'm a bit short.'

'No,' I said and he went back into the house. I hoped I was

right. I was afraid for Dermot but they knew I was in full charge of the shop.

Sometimes when I was awake at night I'd think maybe they'd shoot me and that I'd die. I'd have to hold up my face out of the bedclothes to take a deep breath then because, while I wasn't afraid of the next world or of leaving this one behind, I didn't look forward to the act of dying. 'I wasn't afraid of having babies,' I thought to myself. 'I wasn't a bit nervous. I made no fuss. I wasn't afraid.' Then it occurred to me that it wasn't the same. I couldn't know were the babies frightened. That was the parallel. They left their warm dark womb along a narrow passage with the danger of getting stuck and wanting oxygen. Was the world they fought their way into a wonderful place? It was light, there was that. In the next world would be perpetual light. When I was a wee girl I couldn't say the word. 'Let perpetual light shine upon them' – that was the prayer. 'May they rest in peace. Amen.' We always said that about the dead. 'The Sabbath peace of the people of God' one of the priests used to talk about and it sounded lovely but it was the light I yearned for. I had a kind of a recollection of wakening up once and opening my eyes into such strong sunlight that I had to close them again and I let myself fall back to sleep in the sweetest contentment I have ever known. The strange thing is I can't think how or when it happened to me because no house where I'd slept let in that kind of morning sun. The Belfast streets were too narrow and too shaded and in the country the old aunts' house had little small windows that you couldn't even see out of without bending down. So I have often thought that was my foretaste of Heaven.

'Ah, sure we'll be happy in Heaven,' I said one day in the shop because the women were telling of their troubles, all bowed down. And one of them said, earnestly enough, 'Do you think will we? Will we be happy in Heaven? I often wonder. Because I wouldn't feel at home if I was happy.' And she gave a cackle of a laugh and gathered up her bread and went out.

They didn't shoot me. They knocked at the door one windy night and I answered it. Dermot said we wouldn't open up at all but there was no sense in that. 'We're to burn you out, Mrs,' they said and they shouldered the shop door easily enough. It went up like matchwood.

I never said a word to them but when they came into the house itself and began pouring petrol over my bags of flour and on the floors Dermot started pleading with them. 'Not the house, not the house. It's all I have. You've done the shop. Let that do. It's the shop you've a quarrel with. I never did you no harm. I'll pay anything.'

They just said, 'We've our orders. We have to do what we're told. You know that.' They asked us did we want to get our clothes. 'And a few blankets, Mrs. It's cold out.'

There was a big case in the house Patrick had left behind the last time he was home because it wasn't good enough quality for him. So I packed what I could and stood out in the street and watched my livelihood and habitation disappear in flames flying up into the sky and showers of sparks whirling into the clouds. The only phone in the street was in our house so it was a long time before the fire engine came. Our street is not the easiest to get at if you don't know your way but it didn't matter because nothing of ours could be saved and Stanley had left his house next door empty the previous year so we didn't have to worry about him. At the end of the street where there were a few houses still occupied people were standing out watching but not coming close.

'Where'll we go?' Dermot asked, and I said, 'To Mary Brigid's.'

'It's a long walk,' he said. 'Could we not go to your mother's?'

'I don't want to alarm her,' I said. 'We'll go to Mary Brigid's.'

It was a long walk because the short cuts were shut off with wire to protect the soldiers and the RUC, but we trudged over there with our suitcase and our blankets and we never said a word all the way.

twenty-one

'Oh, Martha!' Mary Brigid said with such sympathy that I felt a cheat because my main feeling was relief that we hadn't been shot. She bustled us in and got ready the boys' bedroom, empty while they were away. Brendan stood around in the background, looking worried. 'Don't get up in the morning till we've gone to school,' Mary Brigid said. 'You need the rest and it would be easier all round. You know where everything is to make your breakfast. I'll take a race home at lunch-time.'

There were two single beds in the room and after we lay down Dermot said, 'Are you warm enough, Martha? You're not shivering? Would you like me to come over and warm you up?'

'No,' I said. 'I'm all right. You just go to sleep.' I heard him snoring in a minute but he wakened dozens of times during the night. I didn't sleep at all. I lay there with my eyes shut and the blazes leaping up against my eyelids. I didn't think of anything about the future or about the past.

In the morning I heard them up and about, Mary Brigid, Emer and little Roisin flying around doing dishes, banging doors and Brendan's heavier footsteps. Then the car started up and the house was quiet.

'I'm going to have a bath,' I said to Dermot. 'And you should have one too. We smell of the fire.' Such luxury it was. I hadn't had a full-sized bath since the hospital where I had the babies. I had a tin bath, of course, that I carried up to my bedroom and filled with a kettle of hot water and a bucket of cold and we were clean afterwards but there was no comfort about it. Mary Brigid's bath was a big white one with claw feet and a roughened surface because it was old. I washed myself and my hair and lay there happily enough. Dermot hovered outside. Three times he asked, 'Are you all right in there, Martha?' What was he so anxious about now, I wondered, now that I was safe in Mary Brigid's lovely house? I laid our breakfast on the kitchen table under the big window that looked out on their garden where the white blossom was just coming out on the top branches of the plum tree and the light in the sky was reflected on wide ivy leaves on its trunk. Into my mind came a picture of the Belfast bus watched across three fields through leafless hedges in the last lonely winter I had spent in the country.

'Will you sit down and eat your breakfast,' I said to Dermot. He wouldn't relax at the table. Of course he had been over to visit there only a few times in all the years we were married.

'I'd like to get away over home,' he said. 'I want to see what we can save. And I suppose I'd better see about reporting it to the police.'

'What do you want to bother with the police for?' I demanded. 'We don't want to get involved with the RUC.'

'Well, will you come and see what's left?' he asked but I told him it would be better for just him to go. I knew there was nothing left worth saving. My bakery was gone. I'd seen it go. He wasn't long gone before he was back in a state, to tell me the bulldozers were in, knocking down all our end of the street, all the empty houses. I said, 'Oh,' and he said, 'Martha, that was my house. That was all I owned in the world.'

'You didn't own it,' I told him. 'You paid rent.'

'It was the same as owning it. We've always owned it. I remember my father in that house.' He was nearly crying. 'You don't care,' he accused me and I shrugged.

'What's done's done,' I said. 'Maybe you should go and find out what we're due in compensation or another house.'

He stood around from one foot to the other until he heard Mary Brigid's car at the gate. Then he bolted.

She came rushing in with grocery bags and started unloading flour and wheatenmeal and soda and cartons of buttermilk on the kitchen table and she laughed. 'I knew there wasn't a dust of flour in the house,' she said. 'I was caught out with not expecting you. There, you'll feel at home now,' and she gave me a clap on the back that turned into a half hug. I had the kettle boiled to make her tea but she hadn't time to take it and I was left alone in the house.

I sat there for a wee while thinking to myself, 'Why did he marry me except just to mind the house? He doesn't care a thing about me. His mother told him to find someone to look after him and the house and I just imagined he wanted me for myself. Anybody would have done him if she would have kept his house the way it was and provided him with clean shirts.' I felt worthless. I got myself into the scullery and made a bit of bread and I thought, 'If I am not baking bread I am nobody and nothing.' Other women might have value because their husbands or their children loved them but my husband didn't care two straws about me, and my children were grown up and gone. Patrick had dropped all the things that I believed in and told me I was no use to them, and who was to say what the others thought. 'I'd better take a run over to my mother's after tea,' I said to myself.

It wasn't tea, of course, that they had at that time. It was their dinner of potatoes with beef and onions and mushrooms in a casserole and a pineapple afterwards. There was no need for the bread at all and Dermot didn't show up until bedtime, so I didn't get to my mother's. He said he had had his meals with Theresa and after a day or two he said he'd sleep there too – it would be handier. He didn't ask me to go with him but to be fair he would have known for sure that I wouldn't go. My mother didn't seem to take in what had happened. She was getting old. She could look after herself but she had no energy over to worry and I didn't insist on pushing mine at her. I was the same again as I had been in my teens in the country – deserted.

I did the same things as I had done then. I cleaned the house, I baked, I did the messages. When either of Mary Brigid's boys came home for a weekend or for the holidays I moved down to the couch in the sitting-room and was in everybody's way. I overheard Emer on the phone one day mentioning me. 'Oh well, I don't know,' she said, 'you see we have this aunt staying with us. It complicates things a bit. Her house was demolished in this urban renewal carry-on and she's waiting for a suitable place to open her business again. She's really weird. She insists it's her duty to provide good wholesome bread for the poor . . . Oh, I know, but it's a bit of a nuisance.' I tiptoed away and clattered in the kitchen.

I remembered teaching her to bake when she was a wee girl and she got into a state, saying, 'I can't do it like you, Martha. Martha, why can't I do it like you?' It turned out that the teaspoon smoothing out the bread soda on the palm of my hand always hit against my wedding ring and she thought the little click was part of the process. I dug out a Hallow Eve ring for her but she said it was no good, it wasn't the real sound. They never called me Auntie, just Martha. I used to love her company when she was small. I had often wished I had a wee girl just like her.

After that phone call I couldn't feel affectionate towards her for a long time and Mary Brigid, I knew, could feel the atmosphere. She and I rubbed each other the wrong way every now and again. The bright pink cheeks she'd kept all along had a purplish tinge with broken veins when you looked close. I was spoiling her life. She had a very comfortable life although maybe she didn't have much time to enjoy it. She had a lovely house and garden and the district she lived in was quiet and content and green from the trees and the golf links. Everybody spoke to everybody else on the avenues and nobody seemed to mind who was Protestant and who was Catholic although Brendan told me that half a dozen houses were put up for sale when a new church was built on a hill overlooking the place and the Angelus bell and the Mass bells rang out every day. Catholics bought these houses because the price had dropped and their small children played on the footpaths. I loved the sound of their little voices.

After a very short time I had no money. I had used up what little there was in the bank. I never made much more than I needed for housekeeping from my bread. I had thought when the boys left home that I would need so much less, that I'd be able to save, but that was when the people began to leave the old houses in our street and my takings went down. Dermot had his dole but he never thought of that as anything but his own private income. Sometimes Mary Brigid left me a five-pound note but I made sure always to spend it on messages for the house. I'd have liked the odd trip into town but I was too proud to use Mary Brigid's money for my own pleasure.

Dermot came to see me when he took the notion. He might come two or three times one week and then not at all for the next fortnight. He came during the day while they were all out and I found myself looking forward to the sound of his footsteps on the front path, and every time their gate creaked I felt my heart lift, thinking it was him. He was looking harassed, getting old. He never criticised Theresa but I couldn't imagine that his life in her house amounted to much. Then one day he came all excited to tell me that the people at the lower end of our street had been provided with mobile homes just outside their old houses so that the whole row could be knocked down and new houses built.

'Could we get one?' I asked before I could stop myself.

'Of course we're going to get one. What do you think I was waiting for?'

How could I know when he had never mentioned anything about it?

The houses were built very quickly, not in straight long streets but round little courtyards. They called them closes. There was no house in just the same position as the old house but once Dermot found out which was to be ours we kept an eye on the building of it. The dump itself was changed too. Where the black tarmacadam playground had been there was now a grand green field with goalposts and the muddy slopes were covered with little shrubs and small trees. It made me laugh to think how they were bribing us. It was nice all the same.

'What will we do for furniture?' I asked Dermot while we were watching the roofs being put on. We were to have a sitting-room and a hall as well as a kitchen downstairs and two bedrooms and a beautiful bathroom upstairs.

'We have our compensation,' he said, and I gaped at him.

'How did you get that?' I asked.

'I've been at it all along. Right from the day after the fire. There's no sense in not getting what you can get. The Sinn Fein advice centre helped me all the way.' I started to laugh and he laughed too after a minute. 'Well, why not?' he said.

'Maybe we should vote for them too,' I said, still laughing.

'We could do worse,' he said. 'They're the only people that scare the Brits.'

Brendan and Mary Brigid would have had a fit if they had heard us. It was all right for them. They never needed help. Nothing happened to them anyway in their nice house in their mixed district and if they wanted information they knew what to do and where to go. We didn't but we were getting a bit cuter. Dermot was told I could never open a bread shop in the front window of our lovely wee house. That wouldn't be proper at all. He was sorry for me when he broke it to me but now that I knew things could be arranged I didn't get too depressed.

I looked at a block of shops up on the front of the road. Three were boarded up, empty, covered with black writing. Some of it was just bad language, other bits were about the Supergrass trials. They weren't too good at spelling perjurer. I wondered how safe I would be there. How long would it be before it was burnt out too unless I subscribed when I was asked? Maybe they had stopped knee-capping. I couldn't be expected to be brave all the time. I couldn't conduct a campaign all on my own.

There was a flourishing fish shop in the block and I called in a few times to talk to the man who ran it. 'Safe?' he said. 'Safe as houses!' When I told him about the house, but not who'd done it, he gave me a free herring and told me he'd protect me – laughing. 'Ach, you'd be all right here. You're in the public gaze here.'

I thought the public were too frightened and turned their heads away and I didn't blame them.

twenty-two

The day we moved into our new house was cold with a wind sweeping down from the Cave Hill. The sitting-room had a fire behind a glass door to heat the water and radiators all over the house and I knew it would be lovely and comfortable later on. But it took a while to warm up the walls and every time the doors were opened by the furniture people and the gas people and the electric people all the warmth I was trying to encourage was torn out. My mother had made curtains for the windows, taking twice the time she'd bargained for, all along losing the measurements. The new table and chairs were lonely in the kitchen.

'You'll have to get all wee ornaments the way we used to have. It's not like home yet,' Dermot said.

'This house is for both of us,' I said. 'It's not your mother's house now. It won't be like that.' He didn't say anything and indeed I had no idea of what kind of a room I wanted. I had no picture in my head of what I would like or not like except I didn't want it to look the same as the old woman's house.

Upstairs we had a new bed with a stiff hard mattress, new bedclothes not cosy yet, new pillows too plump for comfort. In spite of my hot water-bottle I couldn't stop shivering till Dermot got in and put his arms round me. 'I'll keep you warm,' he said. 'Do you remember the way we were so cold on our wedding night?' Afterwards he laughed about 'an old couple like us' and I thought how lucky we were, far luckier than we deserved. 'Sure, you won't leave me again, will you, Martha?' he said.

'I never left you,' I protested. 'It was only that we were burnt out and you wouldn't stay in Mary Brigid's.'

'Oh, you left me, all right,' he said. 'Years ago.'

I tucked the bedclothes in round his back and he went straight off to sleep.

I lay with my eyes closed and the scribbled shutters of the

empty shop came into my mind. I could see how to fix up the shop well enough, even if I couldn't picture my own house. I could think of where to put the counter and the shelves and how to get the bakehouse equipped at the back with ovens and hot-plates and working surfaces and sinks and, behind that, fine steel bins for the meal and flour. Maybe I'd even get a wee girl in and teach her how to bake; so that it could go on when I was too old.

'Dermot,' I said, shaking his shoulder a bit. 'Will you help me to see about a grant or a loan or something to open a new bread shop?'

'I'll do anything at all for you,' he said, only a wee bit awake.

'Anything in the world for you, Martha.' It was not true, of course. He wouldn't even give me any money unless I kept on at him. Maybe he thought it was true, though. At any rate, it was nice to listen to. After all, maybe I don't always face the truth about myself either.

A NOTE ON THE AUTHOR

Mary Beckett was born in Belfast into a family of teachers. She herself taught in Ardoyne in Belfast until her marriage in 1956 when she went to live in Dublin. She began writing short stories when she was twenty-three, first for BBC radio and then for literary magazines in Dublin, Cork and Belfast. She stopped writing for twenty years while rearing two daughters and three sons. In 1980 the Poolbeg Press brought out a collection of her short stories called *A Belfast Woman.*